I0453849

FOOD 4 THOUGHT

RICHARD the POORER'S

Food 4 Thought

SECOND EDITION

A Smorgasbord of Thoughts & Ideas
for Those Who Cogitate on Relationships,
Ideology, Wealth, Power, and More

FOREWORD BY
"BENJAMIN FRANKLIN"

TOM FITZGERALD

acclaimed author of
Beyond Chicken Soup and *Poor Richard's Lament*

the publishing CIRCLE.

Copyright © 2012, 2025 Tom Fitzgerald
All rights reserved.

No part of this publication may be reproduced or transmitted in any form or by any means, mechanical or electronic, including photocopying and recording, or by any information storage and retrieval system without permissions and writing from the publisher (except by a reviewer, who may quote brief passages and/or short brief video clips in a review.)

No part of this publication may be used for training, testing, or developing artificial intelligence systems, machine learning models, or any similar technologies without the express written permission of the author or publisher. Unauthorized use of this content for such purposes is strictly prohibited and may result in legal action.

Send permission requests to the publisher at:
admin@thepublishingcircle.com.
Attention: Permissions Coordinator
Regarding Tom Fitzgerald

DISCLAIMER: The Publisher and the Author make no representations or warranties with respect to the accuracy or completeness of the contents of this work and specifically disclaim all warranties, including without limitations, warranties of fitness for a particular purpose. No warranty may be created or extended by sales or promotional materials. The advice and strategies contained herein may not be suitable for every situation. This work is sold with the understanding that the Publisher is not engaged in rendering medical, legal, accounting, or other professional services. If professional assistance is required, the services of a competent professional person should be sought. Neither the Publisher nor the Author shall be liable for damages arising here from.

The fact that an organization or website is referred to in this work as a citation and/or a potential source of further information does not mean that the Author or Publisher endorses the information the organization or website may provide or recommendations it may make. Further, readers should be aware that Internet websites listed in this work may have changed or disappeared between when this work was written and when it is read. The Publisher is not responsible for the Author's website, other mentioned websites, or content of any website that is not owned by the publisher.

The names of some individuals referenced in this book have been changed to protect and honor their privacy.

All content is the Author's opinion only.

RICHARD THE POORER'S FOOD 4 THOUGHT
SECOND EDITION
ISBN 978-1-955018-95-1 (PAPERBACK)
ISBN 978-1-955018-94-4 (HARDCOVER)
ISBN 978-1-955018-92-0 (LARGE-PRINT PAPERBACK)
ISBN 978-1-955018-93-7 (E-BOOK)

Cover and book design by Michele Uplinger

PRAISE FOR
Richard the Poorer's Food 4 Thought

"The wisdom in this unique offering will help guide and nourish you."
BERNIE S. SIEGEL, MD
AUTHOR OF *Love, Medicine & Miracles* and *Prescriptions for Living*

"Bread fills the belly; wisdom fills the mind; together they feed the soul.
Tom Fitzgerald's *Richard the Poorer's Food 4 Thought* is soul food
like no other. I love this book!"
RABBI DR. RAMI
AUTHOR OF *Recovery, the Sacred Art*

Richard the Poorer's Food 4 Thought is a unique source of nourishment
for mind, body, and soul—the best diet for a healthy life.
MICHEL SUAS
PRESIDENT AND FOUNDER, **San Francisco Baking Institute**

Each page of *Richard the Poorer's Food 4 Thought*
deliciously nourishes the reader. A great way to start or end each day!
JUDITH M. FERTIG
AUTHOR OF *200 Fast & Easy Artisan Bread Recipes*

Richard the Poorer's Food 4 Thought is a treasure.
JACK HAAS, PHD
AUTHOR OF *Seeking Bliss*

Richard the Poorer's Food 4 Thought
is a savory concoction of homespun wisdom.
DR. MARDY GROTHE
AUTHOR OF *Oxymoronica* and other quotation anthologies

In *Richard the Poorer's Food 4 Thought*, Tom Fitzgerald
offers plenty of nourishment.
JAMES GEARY
FORMER EDITOR OF *Time Magazine Europe*
AUTHOR OF *Geary's Guide to the World's Great Aphorists*

Richard the Poorer's Food 4 Thought is special.
Savor it slowly."
JOHN PENBERTHY
AUTHOR OF *To Bee or Not to Bee*

For Jane Joe (JJ) Shea

Foreword

Dear Reader,

The author of this singular volume recently inquired of me whether I might be amenable to associating my name and reputation with it, it being a species of literary work of abiding interest to me. I found myself not only amenable to the gentleman's request, but eager for it, for two reasons:

Firstly, in composing a previous volume, called *Poor Richard's Lament*, the author of the present volume managed, by diligent exercise of his pen, to liberate me from my celestial confinement for near one full day, at the cost to him of nine years of toil and trouble. Futile indeed would be any effort on my part toward unburdening myself of the obligation I feel toward the gentleman for the gift of that single day. Liberty, as in the case of a breeze to the becalmed, is most precious to those who have naught of it.

Secondly, in acceding to the gentlemen's request, I find opportunity to sermonize a little on the subject of improvement, which, at bottom, is the concern of the present volume. Let me begin in this regard by confessing to having been, over the course of my eighty-four years on Earth, a man joined as if by wedlock to the very notion of improvement, not only as such relates to one's self or one's fellows, but also as it relates to various devices, instruments, structures, habits of mind, opinions, norms, and institutions.

Indeed, it has long been my opinion, as informed by a perhaps outsized body of experience, matching perhaps an outsized body of another sort, that there are no bounds on what might, or should be, improved.

One example of my own experience with improvement concerns a deficiency, or better to say, a lack of development, regarding my rhetorical skills. Unfortunately, I had in my youth little access to formal means or methods by which I might improve the effectiveness of my discourse. Fortunately, I possessed wits enough about me to realize that anyone with imagination enough to assay a problem in its fullness must, by way of logical extension, possess imagination enough to conceive a solution to it.

In the present case, the solution consisted of my analyzing arguments found in the occasional magazine that made its way from London to my father's tallow shop in Boston, and then reconstituting those arguments toward improving upon them as regards both the language used and the rhetorical devices employed. The benefit owing to me by way of this exercise exceeded all expectation.

Without improvement indeed—recognizing the need for it, conceiving an appropriate project to effect it, and then executing that project—we and what we individually or collectively make of ourselves, not to mention what we make of the world at large, would be doomed to becoming no greater than a fraction of what we, or it, might otherwise have become. The loss in each case, I submit, would be rendered all the dearer by its avoidability.

What the author offers in this truly singular volume is at least an opportunity to consider anew such beliefs, notions, and aspirations that might be improved upon toward avoiding the avoidable, lest one receive a visit from Madam Regret, with whom, should you have a history anywise resembling my own, you might well have already become well acquainted.

YOUR LOYAL & HUMBLE SERVANT,

B. Franklin, PRINTER

"

At length, I recollected the thoughtless saying of a great princess, who, on being informed that the country people had no bread, replied, "Let them eat cake."

JEAN JACQUES ROUSSEAU
Confessions

I have constantly interspersed moral sentences, prudent maxims, and wise sayings, many of them containing much good sense in very few words, and therefore apt to leave strong and lasting impressions on the memory of young persons, whereby they may receive benefit as long as they live, when both Almanack and Almanack-maker have been long thrown by and forgotten.

POOR RICHARD'S ALMANACK, 1747

Isabel in *The Portrait of a Lady:*
"One should get as many new ideas as possible."

HENRY JAMES, 1881

"

Contents

Meat & Taters

Coffee & Dessert

RICHARD the POORER'S

Food4Thought

SECOND EDITION

Foreword by

'BENJAMIN FRANKLIN'

A Smorgasbord of Thoughts & Ideas
for Those Who Cogitate on Relationships,
Ideology, Wealth, Power, and More

TOM FITZGERALD

acclaimed author of *Beyond Chicken Soup* and *Poor Richard's Lament*

the publishing CIRCLE™

Introduction

R ichard the Poorer's *Food 4 Thought* is a smorgasbord of thoughts and ideas carefully crafted to stimulate cogitation on all manner of topics and issues. For those cogitators who prefer snacky or horsd'oeurvey kinds of fare in this regard, *Food 4 Thought* offers 880 bitesized morsels in the form of what Ben Franklin referred to as "moral sentences, prudent maxims, and wise sayings." These tidy tidbits fall into 57 categories ranging from Anger to Men & Women to Hope & Happiness to Work & Career.

For those cogitators who prefer a little heftier fare, *Food 4 Thought* offers 69 mini-essays on a wide range of topics, from courtship to the state of manhood in America to the real cause behind the obesity pandemic. These "Buns & Biscuits," as they are herein referred, are a page or less in length and are meant to be partaken of one or two at a time. For those cogitators who prefer something heftier still, *Food 4 Thought* offers several hardy entrées. Rounding out *Food 4 Thought*'s salivating fare are several exotic confectionaries.

Bon appétit!

Starters & Snacks

1
Anger

1

Only in rising above our anger can we forgive; only in forgiving can we rise above our anger.

2

Anger acknowledged is information; anger acted upon, error.

3

What a lack of familiarity is to mistrust
a lack of relationship is to road rage.

4

Anger is hate's inebriant, revenge's lubricant.

5

What humiliation is to anger, gasoline is to ember.

6

Give anger its due –
but not the whole of you

7

Anger is the catalyst nature uses to transform the gold of our humanity into the brass of our brutality.

8

Anger is energy for good or for ill; it is never just energy.

9

No quicker to regret than on the back of rage.

10

Anger and ignorance have no ear for reason.

11

Count your fingers, thumb to thumb—
or end up looking pretty darn dumb.

12

What anger composes, the Cancel button disposes.

13

Fantasy allows us to do harmlessly what anger would have us do regretfully.

14

Almost everything stitched in anger needs to be pulled out and started over.

2
Arrogance

15

The best cure for an inflation of ego is a pinprick of humility.

16

Arrogance is like a suit of armor; it makes us perfectly invulnerable until such time we need to relieve ourselves.

17

Arrogance, as in the case of the vampire, tends not to reflect in any of the mirrors into which it peers.

18

Arrogance is a liberal defining a problem and prescribing the solution; a conservative judging the problem and condemning the cause.

19

The only legitimate reason humankind has to judge itself superior is its ability to puff up feathers it does not have.

20

Arrogance is the ego's Viagra.

21

We can only be as arrogant or as alcoholic as those around us will allow us to be. It's all their fault!

22

If we were truly made in the image of God, wouldn't it show?

23

Ignorance is belief without basis; arrogance, belief as basis.

24

Arrogance is claiming dominion over the fish of the sea, and over the fowl of the air, and over the cattle, and over all the earth, and over every creeping thing. Self-destruction is the same thing.

25

Arrogance is to a weak, over-educated person what machismo is to a weak, under-educated person.

26

Arrogance is fertile of tongue, fallow of ear.

27

Children are not born with attitude; they are allowed it.

3
Art, Beauty & Creativity

28
A creative mind is the quill pen of a rebellious spirit.

29
If beauty is "in the eye of the beholder," why bother with makeup?

30
Every soul is a womb; every artist, a midwife.

31
The creative mind is adolescent one moment, adult the next.

32
Lincoln wrote the Gettysburg address because Lincoln was the Gettysburg address. Martin Luther King wrote the "I Have a Dream" speech because Martin Luther King was the "I Have a Dream" speech. Art is the artist.

33
All great art is contrived to bring notice not to the artist but to the art.

34
Time was when a rambunctious creativity was not only tolerated but encouraged. Today it's put on Ritalin.

35
What city viewed by night does not disappoint by day.

36
One way to be beautiful is to treat yourself as if you were.

37
What wings are to the butterfly, imagination is to the soul.

38

There used to be no app for art. Now we have AI. Pity.

39

Creativity goes boldly where conventionality fears to tread.

40

Beauty is of two kinds—that which appeals to the senses (Dresden burning by night), and that which appeals to the soul (an eagle soaring in flight).

41

A practiced silence is the hobgoblin of a reluctant imagination.

42

The appeal of the art is proportionate to the passion of the artist.

43

The bottle that holds the genie of our creativity is either corked or uncorked; it is never empty.

44

Art that doth not honor symmetry, art not.

4

Capitalism / Socialism

45

Socialism is like free love; it sounds good on paper, but it never seems to work out very well.

46

We need capitalism to be something more than survival of the fittest; socialism to be something less than survival of the sickest.

47

Once capitalism has killed off all the competition, who's going to bury the dead?

48

Capitalism presupposes boundless growth and infinite resources; socialism presupposes infinite charity and boundless goodwill. Do we need to do some further presupposing, do you suppose?

49

An unregulated market is like a four-way intersection without a traffic light.

50

No economy based on greed can lead to anything other than moral bankruptcy. No economy based on good intentions can lead to anything other than fiscal bankruptcy.

51

Capitalism is like a tumor that grows until it has sucked up all the sustenance around it, ensuring itself of its own demise.

5
Courage

52

We embrace truth not so much with our reason as with our courage.

53

Character is what it takes to admit our mistakes to ourselves; courage, what it takes to admit our mistakes to others.

54

Much of what is held up as raw courage is actually parboiled stupidity.

55

Any run-of-the-mill coward can avoid blame; only the truly craven can pin it on somebody else.

56

The most precious of mettles is courage.

57

A coward is a friend to every man, hence to no man.

58

Courage is what it takes to be the only one who isn't when everybody else is.

59

Courage comes easiest to those with the least to lose.

60

We are courageous to the extent we will risk humiliating ourselves.

61

A mob is solidarity one moment, stampede the next.

62

Least forgivable is the cowardice of complicity.

6
Death

63

Death wouldn't be half such a fright,
were we allowed a rehearsal,
before opening night.

64

Most of us carry on as if we were going to live forever;
denial, not religion, is the true opiate of the masses.

65

In adolescence, we defy death; in adulthood, ignore it; in
old age, embrace it.

66

All but death can be overcome with a fierce tenacity of
spirit; even it, though, can be much delayed.

67

Squeeze a few drops of mortality into a beaker half-
filled with self-awareness and religion is the precipitate.

68

Time can abate the pain; never the ache.

69

In the absence of death, life would be all pulp, no juice.

70

Hell is being fitted at the moment of our death with a
chain forged of all the moments of our lives we wasted
dishonoring the miracle of our being.

71

The process of dying ends when we stop breathing;
it begins when we stop trying.

72

Death is when we reach into the jar of second chances
and find it empty.

73

We fear death to the extent we realize we have not yet lived.

74

In death, the great equalizer is the casket;
in life, the commode.

7
Democracy

75

Democracy presumes not so much that human beings can govern themselves, but that they can deny themselves.

76

Freedom fosters democracy; democracy, dependency.

77

Democracy is born of enlightenment and cooperation; dies of ignorance and alienation.

78

The Achilles Heel of every form of government known to man is its inability to anticipate.

79

Compromise does not forestall ruin; it delays it.

80

When the ayes have it, the nays only pretend not to.

81

There's a reason there are no pure democracies in the world.

82

The USA is not a democracy; not even close. It's a republic, and barely that.

83

The only form of pure democracy still existent in America today is the town meeting.

8
Envy & Jealousy

84
Where envy ends, enmity begins.

85
Envy wants a friend.

86
Envy is schizophrenic—enmity one day, emulation the next.

87
Envy is the infant; jealousy, the adult.

88
Envy urges action; jealously, theft.

89
Had the Wicked Witch envied no further than her nose, the brothers Grimm would have had to compose a very different strain of prose.

90
A democracy can thrive only where men of good will do.

9
Ethics & Morality

91

A liar must possess in memory what he lacks in conscience.

92

Desire is the undoing of all virtue, and not a few waistlines.

93

Ethics emanate from empathy; empathy, from intimacy.

94

When we too much want something, we will too much pay for it.

95

Law is elevation of order over chaos
Morality, elevation of restraint over impulse
Ethics, elevation of other over self

96

The Golden Rule derives not from a burning bush but from a double helix.

97

Better to pick a pocket than betray a trust.

98

There is no sacred rule or divine decree that even the most righteous amongst us would not violate given the right set of circumstances.

99

The worst thing about lying is that we usually end up believing our own lies.

100

The rabbis have it right—it all depends.

101

To hate, as to think, is neither good nor bad. 'Tis what we do with our hate, as with our thoughts, that is either good or bad.

102

Being honest is like paddling upstream. It's a helluva lot easier not to and we can't take even a moment's break without backsliding.

103

What ambition is to prevarication desire is to purloinacation.

104

When we cease being a community of moral deliberators, we cease being a community.

105

Our behavior depends on what we value; what we value, on what we hold to be our purpose.

106

Sometimes the ends justify the means, sometimes they do not. The moral duty of mankind is to divine the difference.

107

What oozy little pustule is not the fester of a larger corruption?

10
Existence

108

The only miracle greater than the existence of us is the existence of existence.

109

The circle is the only geometry.

110

Zero is the egg of all possibility.

111

All measurement is approximate; all boundary, illusion.

112

As there can be no odd without even, no minus without plus, no up without down, so there can be no nothing without something.

113

No event can create itself.

114

Time cannot begin; nor end.

115

In the grand scheme of things, what is possible is inevitable.

116

Order is the act; chaos, the intermission.

117

Beginnings and endings are the stuff of theology; circles and cycles, the stuff of philosophy.

118

Logic is both the chicken and the egg—nothing can precede it; nothing can supersede it.

119

In the eye of Finitude, there is time because there is distance, distance because there is separation. In the eye of Infinitude, there is only the eye.

120

Daddy, if the universe is still expanding, where is all the new space coming from?
Go ask your Mother.

121

Only what is finite can behold what is finite; it takes one to know one.

122

As there are four cardinal points of direction, so there are four cardinal realms of reality—the logical, the mathematical, the physical, and, for lack of a better term, the mystical.

123

Nonexistence is the eternal absence of possibility; existence, the eternal presence of possibility.

124

It all sums to zero—but doesn't.

125

Space is not nothing; only nothing is.

126

It's turtles all the way down, unless, of course, you believe in hell, in which case it's snapping turtles all the way down.

11
Fame & Celebrity

127

To pursue fame is to seek the attention we never got when we most needed it.

128

As in the case of facelifts and tummy tucks, fame and celebrity can only be envied from a distance.

129

Those most likely to achieve an enduring fame are those least likely to seek it.

130

Fame is the mirage when our thirst is for meaning.

131

When fame is the harvest, the humus is not humility.

132

Inside every adult seeking adulation is a child still coming home to an empty house.

133

We place celebrities on pedestals because we can only worship what we cannot reach.

12
Family & Parenthood

134

If it takes a village to raise a child, what happens when there are no villages?

135

Why do the rest of us need to know that you are "Proud of (y)our honor student?"

136

If home is where they have to take us in, what if we never moved out?

137

Loving parents are the children of loving parents; like begets like.

138

Children don't make very good pets.

139

Children come with the capacity for courtesy but not the inclination.

140

Parents who relinquish their role as teachers are destined to learn a lesson or two.

141

If you succeed, share your success with your child; it will cheer you both. If you fail, share your failure with your child; it will comfort you both.

142

One of our greatest errors as parents is to fail to give our children permission to be who they cannot other than be.

143

A spoiled child is like a plant kept too long in its starter pot.

144

To protect our children from suffering the consequences of their actions is to protect only ourselves.

145

Almost every dark corner in a child can be traced back to a burned-out bulb in a parent.

146

Few amusements provide more entertainment to a child than a stack of used printer paper and a box of crayons.

147

Behind every out-of-control lad is an out-of-the-picture dad.

148

Those who fail to discipline their children will be disciplined by them.

149

Those most smiled upon as children are those least likely to aspire to become standup comedians.

150

An infant is what his genes are; a child, what his home is.

151

To awaken to the wails of a hungry infant is to rediscover the splendor of dawn.

152

Is it social media that is destroying family life, or is it the absence of an adult finger on the off button?

153

We can forgive anything in our children except what reminds us of the worst in ourselves.

154

Those who relate best to children are those who best remember what it was like to be small, powerless, and alone.

155

To see our children succeed, we need only give them our time. To see them fail, we need only give them our wealth.

156

The child who takes the life of another, and the child who takes his own, are the same child.

157

Wishful thinking and feminist theology to the contrary, parenthood is a full-time job.

158

Children live in their imagination, some never leave.

13
Freedom & Autonomy

159
Half of freedom is being allowed to make mistakes. The other half is taking responsibility for those mistakes.

160
Nothing is coerced; to act is to acquiesce.

161
We are free not to the degree we satisfy our wants, but to the degree we have no wants to satisfy.

162
When we pay too little for freedom we get even less.

163
No one has become master of his own fate who has not favored questions over answers.

164
There is an abundance of freedom only where there is an abundance of abundance.

165
There are two ways to get out of a hole—wait for someone to come along and figure out the first; close our eyes and imagine the second.

166
If we listen only to those voices we wish to hear, soon there will be no others.

167
Every freedom can be denied us but two—the freedom to think for ourselves, the freedom to feel for others.

168
What desire does not become a shackle; what shackle, not a master?

169

Free will is like the Cheshire cat; it's there, but isn't.

170

There might not be a good choice, but there is always a choice.

171

Liberty, as in the case of a breeze to the becalmed, is most precious to those who have naught of it.

172

Too little freedom is a bad thing and requires remedy. Too much freedom is an even worse thing and defies remedy.

173

If free speech does not include yelling "Fire!" in a theatre, can gun ownership include carrying a pistol into a bar?

14
Friendship & Hospitality

174
Friendship is being there even when it's inconvenient.

175
We can be admired by most, befriended by many, but loved by only a few.

176
The rarest of gems is the listener.

177
Cross-stitched into every successful marriage is the anchor floss of an enduring friendship.

178
Every friendship begins with a mutual willingness to risk.

179
No one warm is ever left out in the cold.

180
If a man's best friend is his dog, pity them both.

181
We are welcoming to strangers to the extent they either bear us gifts or look like us—in that order.

182
The more friends, the fewer intimates; the more intimates, the fewer friends.

183
Friendship is a Dagwood made up of three layers— mutual trust, shared experience, and reciprocal regard. The pickle is optional.

184

What kind of friend we are is revealed by whether we are as willing to listen to troubles as to tell them.

185

No one poor has a penny certain; no one rich, a friend certain.

186

Give me a friend, a glass of wine, a chunk o' cheese
Add a little birdsong, if you would please.

187

As rare as rubies are the friends who do not judge us.

15
God, Religion & Spirituality

188

Religion is a room with a door and a window; spirituality is the window.

189

If God has a plan, we don't.

190

There are as many gods as religions; as many religions as believers.

191

Superstition is a willing servitude.

192

The Catholic Church makes morality, like, real simple. Either your indulgences are, like, paid up, or they are not.
The true believer is ever in doubt.

193

We are the slaves of our biology
 and of our ideology –
but the clowns of our theology

194

God can't remove the water from the sea, because God is the water in the sea.

195

Why is it when we survive a calamity, it's divine intervention, but when others do, it's dumb luck?

196

When was the last time a miraculous cure involved the spontaneous regeneration of a missing finger?

197

Mommy, why would an all-powerful God create a bunch of bumpkins, endow them differently, place them in unequal circumstances, and cast the vast majority of them into hellfire for doing exactly what he had to know they would do?

Go ask your Father.

198

Anxiety is the cost of self-awareness; religion, the consequence.

199

Dogmatism is an excuse not to think; fundamentalism, an imperative not to.

200

If a strange man and a pregnant woman showed up at your door smelling of donkey and perspiration and asked for lodging for the night, would you let them in?

201

The unknowable is the mother of all mythology.

202

The truly religious are those who stand in awe before the ineffable majesty of all that is.

203

Constructing a theology on a false premise is like building a castle on a single point—ever more minions are needed to add ever more ramparts to one side and the other until such time the whole contraption topples over of its own impossibility.

204

Nothing troubles a good Christian more than an even better non-Christian.

205

The Shakers embraced celibacy and now there are no Shakers. Is there a lesson here?

206

If we were able to bear the truth about Santa Claus, why not the truth about the one for whom Santa Claus is surrogate?

207

Religion tends to center on accountancy; spirituality, on generosity.

208

Can you imagine a living hell worse than living forever?

209

Dogma, like flypaper, tends to attract those who can't quite see it for what it is.

210

Where hope sags, religion props.

211

Paradise is where we can watch the circus from the bleachers instead of having to jump through hoops.

212

The more painful this life, the more compelling the next.

213

Would a Wickedpedia be free or would we have to pay for it?

214

If there were truly a just god, wouldn't lightning naturally seek out the bigot?

215

A true sovereign favors not the subject who bows and scrapes and utters a deep sigh, but the one who stands straight and tall and looks him in the eye.

216

Daddy, if all living things came from the same Eve cell, how come only humans are made in the image of God? Go ask your Mother.

217

Is it our soul that lusts after eternal life, or is it some other part of us?

218

Should we look also before we take a leap of faith?

219

Each of us has not a soul, but soul; just as each of us has not a purpose, but purpose.

220

Why is it that when a puffed-up prince invokes the divine right of kings, we tweak his nose and give his armor a ding, but when a puffed-up prelate invokes the divine right of kings, we lick his boots and kiss his ring?

221

If we view Little Red Riding Hood as innocence incarnate, and the big bad wolf as evil incarnate, how long before we rid the planet of every wolf?

222

What is most troubling about zealots is not their belief that what is good for them is good for everybody, but their insistence upon it.

223

Religion derives of fear; reverence, of awe.

224

Humility is to spirituality what zealotry is to religion.

225

Mommy, why does God enter into special covenants with white people, but not with black people, brown people, red people, or yellow people?
Go ask your Father.

226

Only in America could Buddhism become another form of narcissism.

227

A religion is not what it preaches but what it practices.

228

If God is the creator of all things, did he create himself?

16

Government, Law & Politics

229
The number of laws required is exponentially proportional to the amount of alienation accumulated.

230
Populism is the last gasp of a failed democracy.

231
The mass of men are willing to be governed by others because they know they are incapable of governing themselves.

232
In business, "good enough" means profit enough; in government, deficit enough.

233
Rule by law is an admission of failure.

234
The problem with government is that it is itself ungovernable.

235
Public office is the feeding trough of the insatiable ego.

236
People give up on the democratic process not because they have been made cynical by it, but because they have been made invisible by it.

237
The realist rules; the idealist rues.

238
A conservative is a liberal whose parents are no longer paying the bills.

239

The only form of governance anticipated by nature is the benevolent dictatorship.

240

The less a politician has to say, the more he says.

241

Only the self-sufficient can afford to be belligerent.

242

Religion aspires to its highest level of intolerance, government, to its highest level of incompetence.

243

Good behavior derives not so much from a fear of retaliation as from a terror of rejection.

244

If only men could be elected "chief," and only women could vote, would we be any worse off than we are now?

245

The rabble is ruleable only because it has not yet discovered the power of numbers.

246

A conservative and a liberal join a book group . . .

17
Maturity / Growing Up

247
There comes a time when we can no longer blame our parents or circumstances for what we are or are not.

248
Being all growed up is stuffing a wrapper in a pocket instead of dropping it on the ground.

249
Too much responsibility squeezes the fun out of us; too little respite prevents it from creeping back in.

250
Childhood is longing to enter that magical realm where all things uncertain become certain, all things inaccessible become accessible, all things unknown become known. Adulthood is pretty much the same thing.

251
The process of growing up begins when we notice the person standing at the center of the universe is not us.

252
Maturity is remaining seated until they call your row.

253
A child's greatest fear is to be abandoned; an adult's, to be rejected; an elder's, to be ignored.

254
Grown-up is a relative term.

255
Golden-fleeced angels and rosy-cheeked cherubs are teddy bears by another name.

256

Maturity is when we recognize need to fit bit and bridle to the me and mine of us.

257

A child is a bundle of excesses; an adult, a bundle of excuses.

18
Heroes & Role Models

258
When everybody is a hero, nobody is.

259
The higher the pedestal, the harder the fall.

260
To worship a hero is to worship ourselves as we would like to be.

261
Is there anything more former than a former hero?

262
From 3 to 13, every boy needs his father to be a hero; from 13 to 21, a fool; from 21 on, a buddy.

263
The meek are today's fools, tomorrow's heroes; the macho, today's heroes, tomorrow's fools.

264
Can a hero in platform shoes still be a hero?

265
Fantasy is where we go to be a hero when we can be one no place else.

266
Not needing a hero is being one's own.

267
To worship a hero from a distance is to see no warts.

268
The main difference between yesterday's hero and today's is today's can post a selfie.

19
Hope & Happiness

269
Happiness is a side effect. Meaning is the mission.

270
The better part of happiness is an abiding absence of unhappiness.

271
We are content to the extent we have no wants;
happy to the extent we have no desires.

272
Fill our balloon with hope and sky's the limit.

273
Happiness is the quality of the moment; the quality of the moment, the quality of us.

274
Fortunately, hope springs eternal; unfortunately, we do not.

275
Happiness derives not from what we possess, attain, or consume, but from who we are in belief, attitude, and behavior.

276
The wise farmer celebrates not when he hears a rumble, but when he feels the rain.

277
Gratification is to the body what fulfillment is to the soul.

278
Give an addict hope today and tomorrow will pretty much take care of itself.

279

If pleasure has no meaning in the absence of pain, pain no meaning in the absence of pleasure, what are we to make of eternal bliss?

280

We cannot be truly happy, unselfconsciously happy, on the superficial levels of self. Not money, not office, not career, not sex, not stuff, not food, not travel, not even sweet revenge can bring us anything more than fleeting flashes of ecstasy—bombs bursting in air, temporarily transforming inner darkness into artificial day.

281

We have largely limited happiness in our time to what we experience over the middle three days of a five-day vacation.

282

A lottery ticket is a toehold on hope.

283

Happiness is not the heat and glare of fanned flames, but a single ember glowing within, warming us evenly, bringing no notice to itself.

284

The sweetest of confections is certainty; first runner-up is hope.

285

Oil may fuel the world, money may make the world go round, but what is oil, what is money, in the absence of hope?

286

Meaning is the ember; fulfillment, the glow.

287

Happiness is not a pot of glitter at the end of the rainbow but the rainbow itself.

288

The foundation of all true contentment is an abiding certainty that one matters.

289

Even laurels can wilt.

290

Hope is the stirrup we use to climb into the saddle of each new day.

291

A hedonist is he who, when he feels a deep yearning, orders another donut.

292

One cannot be simultaneously content and aware of what time it is.

293

The dread felt at first waking is exponentially proportional to the commute waiting.

294

Hope is happiness enough.

295

The young tend to seek happiness in the future; the old, in the past; the wise, in the moment.

296

To pursue the sweet is to risk the sour.

297

To choose the devil we know is to presume all the others unknowable.

298

An alarm clock can only wake us; it can't get us out of bed.

299

Possibility is the mother of all hope.

300

Tomorrow might be another day, but today is all we have.

301

Happiness is not a candy store of dipped blisses and frosted ecstasies in some super mall in the sky, but a smile spread over the ocean of our soul, in the moment of our death.

302

Our level of contentment depends on the amount we have in relation to the amount we need; our level of disappointment, on the amount we lack in relation to the amount we seek.

303

Like the rings on a tree, happiness accumulates a little at a timer, and more in some seasons than in others.

20
Human Nature

304
As certain as death and taxes are the flaws and shortcomings we are disposed to notice in everyone except ourselves.

305
Break a man's leg, he'll walk with a cane.
Break a man's spirit, he'll walk no more.

306
The smaller the village, the fewer the locks.

307
Misery seeks company; shame, solitude.

308
Desperation makes beggars of us all.

309
To know the man, open his refrigerator.

310
Pride-bound today, hide-bound tomorrow.

311
Bigness must fail;
intimacy, you see,
doth not scale

312
If puffballs were to choose the most beautiful puffball of all, would they choose one round and fat, or one lean and tall?

313
Innocent eyes are seeing eyes.

314

The nobility of humanity lies not so much in its ability to create things as in its ability to imagine them.

315

If we are what we do, and do what we believe, and believe what we're told to believe, who are we?

316

While some of us plunge headlong into a swamp of self-deception and quickly drown, most of us wander into a quicksand of wishful thinking and slowly sink.

317

History repeats because people do.

318

The rarest of doors is the one bearing no lock.

319

What political correctness would have us be, human nature will not allow.

320

The reason we tend to prefer pets over people is because pets don't break our hearts until the very end.

321

At birth, we are a handful of possibilities scattered over a small plot of ground; thereafter, we are whatever takes root.

322

Fortunate are those creatures that push our cute button.

323

A nation will suffer equal the folly whether the liberals are in power or the conservatives, the Catholics or the Protestants, the socialists or the capitalists. Ineptitude bears no label.

324

Jefferson's first draft: All men are created equal, with the following exceptions . . .

325

We are gened to genuflect.

326

In the absence of coercion, most of us lack either the will or the discipline to become all we are capable of becoming.

327

We can feel no agony that someone has not felt before us, wrestle no doubt that someone has not wrestled before us, suffer no disappointment that someone has not suffered before us. Fortunately, we can act otherwise.

328

Our dual nature is reflected in our being as eager to see a building razed as raised.

329

No sooner do we mount one peak than we turn to the next. It's not the conquest we seek but the climb.

330

What loose tooth cannot be tortured unto a glorious respite?

331

Lose a mere bauble into a public toilet and we give it up for lost. Lose a diamond ring into the same toilet and . . . how many carats did you say?

332

Our demons dwell not in our heart, or in our soul, but in our medulla oblongata.

333

The new physics: Absent an oppositional force, the gravitational pull of the human ego will accumulate a mass of self-importance until such time it implodes into a singularity of infinite insufferability.

334

More than failure, more than humiliation, more even than death itself, we fear rejection.

335
We are born with the capacity to think for ourselves but with the inclination to let somebody else do it.

336
Trying to reach a closed mind with reasoned argument is lot like trying to count stars on a cloudy night.

337
One cures psychic pain, not by anesthetizing it, but by antagonizing it.

338
If the passive voice were called the craven voice, would mistakes still be made?

339
But for adversity we would never realize our possibility.

340
If we can hold only seven bits of information in our brains at any one time, and only two things in our hands at any one time, what does it mean to multitask?

341
A humiliated enemy is a defeated enemy.

342
Can a gold mine and a golden mind be pretty much the same thing?

343
A child seen by none will one day be seen by all.

344
The problem with conspiracy theories is there is no way all the conspirators could keep their mouths shut.

21
Humility

345

If there was a Nobel Prize for Humility, who would accept it?

346

We're told we can't really love anyone else until or unless we can love ourselves. But isn't it the other way around?

347

Humility is the last lesson learnt, the first forgot.

348

Either invite Humility through the front door or she will enter through the back. She is not proud.

349

There is a special kind of humility known only to the parents of a dying child.

350

Does having "dominion over every living thing" include slaughtering rhinos for their tusks?

351

The truly humble seek not public office but personal service.

352

Humility comes to women by way of birthright; to men by way of two cardiac infarctions and a double bypass.

353

Hair needs a comb, not a mirror.

354

A humble child is the grace of humble parents.

355

When ambition tries to muscle its way to the front of the line, it's humility that can stand in the way.

356

Invisibility and humility are cousins, not blood brothers.

22
Humor

357
A giggle in the morning, a howl at night,
keeps them buzzards, right outa sight.

358
He who laughs last laughs alone.

359
Are conservatives born without a sense of humor or do
they lose it through lack of use?

360
Humor is the sweet that cloaks the bitter.

361
The most important part about being funny is knowing
when not to be.

362
When all else fails, try tickling your feet with your
eyelashes.

363
The best way to avoid being laughed at by others is to
beat them to the punch.

364
To remind yourself of just how much we need each
other, try having a good yuk with your yorkie.

365
If someone tells a joke in a forest, do the trees fall down
laughing?

366
If neither cross nor clove will keep those pesky vampires
at bay, try telling them the one about the vampire who
died of blood poisoning.

367

Laughing one's self to death would seem to preclude any
need for a wake.

23
Ideology

368
An ideologue is like a marionette—all strings, no brains.

369
Ideology is truth by alchemy.

370
When ideology masquerades as pedagogy, good intention as good sense, every child gets left behind.

371
Parkinson's Corollary: Every ideology seeks to fill the available space.

372
The problem with ideology is it tends to be a little heavy on ology, and a little light on idea.

373
Hell on earth: Being stuck in an elevator with two ideologues and a zealot.

374
Too much of what is born of philosophy dies of ideology.

24
Justice

375

Justice is like a hybrid rose; it exists nowhere in the universe in a natural state.

376

No justice, no peace.

377

Justice would be sweet indeed if those who cried "nigger" or "faggot" were reincarnated as both.

378

To quell the conflict, jack up the justice.

379

Justice is either-or; either you get it or you don't.

380

An apology is never quite justice enough.

381

The bane of many a parent is a nine-year-old with an unerring sense of justice.

382

All justice is local.

25
Knowledge & Education

383
A man's best friend is his teacher.

384
Either there is a rational explanation behind every phenomenon, or there is no phenomenon.

385
Where there are too many people to educate, there will be too little education.

386
Ignorance is the worst of evils for it is the witch's brew of all others.

387
"Failing" schools are a symptom, not a cause.

388
Young people are educated not by being subjected to another reform program, but by being instilled with an abiding love of learning.

389
What willful embrace of ignorance is not a wanton display of arrogance?

390
Easy it is to ride a pony of belief; not so easy a bronco of doubt.

391
Half of knowing is knowing who to ask.

392
A mind that produces no grapes yields no wine.

393
The highest education is an understanding of one's self.

394

Knowledge is like the seedless orange; it continues to exist only if we go out of our way to cultivate it.

395

Judge a teacher not by how much she teaches you, but by how much she inspires you to teach yourself.

396

The oak grows tallest where the soil runs deepest.

397

Knowledge in the whole is power; in part, peril.

398

In saving us from the boredom of Eden, did not Eve grace us with a Garden of Readin'?

399

Beware of all mountain tops requiring no ascendance.

400

Our imagination can rearrange pieces of experience; it cannot create them.

401

Acknowledging our mistakes is the bronze; learning from them, the silver; anticipating them, the gold.

402

Economics studied is supply-and-demand; lived, fear-and-greed.

403

We are entitled not to an education, but to a library card.

404

Half of what we think we know is dead wrong; the other half is in the ICU.

405

The quality of an education depends little on the quality of the teachers, less on the quality of the textbooks, least on the quality of the classrooms. The quality of an education depends on the quality of those being educated.

406

If someone tells you they have a PhD in education, run!

407

If every child is special, none is.

408

A liberal education is about asking questions, not about getting answers.

409

Enlightenment is a choice; likewise, ignorance.

410

Every Dark Age begins with attacks on the purveyors of truth. There is no requirement there be an end.

26
Leadership

411
Where there are no philosophers, there are no leaders.

412
In the beginning, it's the word; thereafter, the deed.

413
What the firing squad is to the freedom fighter, false witness is to the truth teller.

414
Leadership is one part vision, one part courage, two parts humility, simmered over the steady heat of a compassionate heart.

415
The true leader runs not for office but from it.

416
As long as public office continues to attract takers over leavers, most of us will continue to get taken.

417
Swagger does not a silverback make.

418
A politician tells us what we want to hear; a leader, what we will hold against him in the next election.

419
Leadership not reluctant is not.

420
What politicians lack in modesty and imagination, they more than make up for in glibness and guile.

421
The common denominator of all politicians is ambition; of all leaders, humility.

422
Politicians are elected; leaders, summoned.

423
A leader stands in front of the flag; a politician, behind it.

424
Beware: Not all pied pipers play the same tune.

425
Politicians are egoists; leaders, egoless.

426
Who will lead the world if Joe and Jane will not?

27
Life

427
Each of us has won the greatest lottery of them all, against the greatest of odds . . . life.

428
Life is like riding a horse—it's painless to the extent we move in rhythm to it, and the faster we go the shorter our time in the saddle is likely to be.

429
From nature's point of view, the purpose of life is life; from our point of view, it's the quality of that life.

430
Life is three-quarters coming to terms with and one quarter settling for.

431
Each of us shares in common with every other living thing on earth a core essence deserving of unconditional reverence and compassion. For this reason, and this reason alone, we should never punish a life by terminating it.

432
Like nuggets of gold, life is cheap in proportion to the amount of it laying around.

433
Life is like a pair of knitting needles and a skein of yarn –partly what we are given to work with, mostly what we make of it.

434
Life is like a great ocean on which float temporal little bubbles of miraculous opalescence.

435

Life is possible, therefore is.

436

The moments of life are like a bag of M&Ms—too little savored until the last one.

437

For one thing to live, others must die. Life is a thousand thank-yous.

28
Loneliness

438
To be self-aware is to know despair.

439
In refusing to risk intimacy, we set our table for one.

440
One form of aloneness
 should never be—
Your child coming home
 to absence of thee

441
When loneliness is the ache, desperation is the agony.

442
In filling our memory with the smiles we gave others, we ensure ourselves against dying alone.

443
Loneliness is a vale of tears; despair, the Grand Canyon.

29
Love & Compassion

444

If there is no greater love "than a man lay down his life for his friend," what is it for a man to lay down his life for a stranger?

445

To be an accountant in matters of love is to be one's only client.

446

Love will die first in the chambers of governance, last in the bosom of motherhood.

447

All true charity is anonymous.

448

There is indeed something that can travel faster than the speed of light . . . love.

449

Tough love is the greater.

450

How we received love as children is how we give it as adults.

451

Adulation is never quite love enough.

452

Love is not only saying you're sorry; it's saying you're sorry even if it wasn't your fault.

453

Love is here today only if it is here tomorrow.

454

Romantic love is nature's alternative to grand theft eroto.

455

A single rose is an expression of love; a dozen, an admission of guilt.

456

To be lovable is to be loved.

457

Love is not saying so; love is doing so.

458

No love is more conditional than romantic love,
None more unconditional than maternal love.

459

Where there are too many people to care about, there will be too little care.

460

Love is the ultimate risk, the ultimate reward.

461

The less churlish, the more cherished.

462

If we adulate those who sacrifice their lives believing an eternal reward awaits, how are we to regard those who sacrifice their lives believing nothing awaits?

463

Romantic love is to epidermis as mother love is to marrow.

30
The Masters

464

Trying to absorb Emerson's commentaries is a bit like trying to hold water on parched ground long enough for it to soak in.

465

If James Joyce had allowed himself to discover the majesty of punctuation, we might have discovered the majesty of his writing.

466

Most great writers of the day
have way too much to say,
but, of course, say it anyway

467

When a writer's empathy is larger than his ego, reading his lines is an easy go.

468

Shakespeare's characters don't speak; they speechify.

469

Cut half the prose from Moby Dick and you'd still have one whale of a tale.

470

If all those great writers are so great, how come we have to read each line four times over to "get it?"

471

Genius is like a peat fire. It smolders below the surface until you start messing with it.

472

Shakespeare had his time. It's over.

31
Men

473

Every father wants a son; needs a daughter.

474

"Gentle-man" is as much an oxymoron as "gentle-women" is a redundancy.

475

Many a barbecue burns because beer does not.

476

What men once derived from carrying a spear they now get from packing a smartphone.

477

We have marriage because males do not take naturally to monogamy; we have divorce because males do not take naturally to marriage.

478

Honk your horn at a man and he'll flip you the bird. Suggest to a man he needs help and he'll dis you. Remind a man of his age and he'll take a mistress. Ignore a man and he'll run for office. Remind a man of how big and important he is and he'll be your friend forever.

479

Manhood is measured not in maidens bedded or money amassed, but in sacrifices made.

480

As long as the mass of men view life as an arena in which one either wins or loses, nothing will change.

481

Trace the Nile of male rage back to its source and you will find a thousand tributaries of shame and humiliation.

482

If it's OK for men to cry, it has to be equally OK for them not to.

483

To understand the reluctance of men to ask for directions, one must appreciate the fact that not so long ago there was no one to ask.

484

It has become fashionable in our time to blame male violence on every social ill except the only one that matters—our collective failure to bless boys into the community of men.

485

What men need most today they used to get without having to make complete fools of themselves.

486

Will Rogers once said he never met a man he didn't like. The only conclusion one can logically draw from this statement is that Mr. Rogers must have lived in a house of mirrors.

487

Can you imagine a daycare run by men? How long before the kiddie art comes off the walls and a big-screen TV goes up?

32
Men & Women

488

We are gendered by our genes, not by our politics.

The human male is a sexual being first, a nurturing being second. The human female is a nurturing being first, a sexual being third.

489

Women expect protection; men, service.

490

What women possess in adaptability men surpass in offendability.

491

Masculinity tends to fill a room; femininity, to furnish it.

492

Women die of a lack of intimacy; men, of a lack of purpose.

493

Why are so many women blonde, so many men bald?

494

Boys are born wild and need to be tamed; girls are born tame and need to be wilded.

495

No gaggle of ganders has any business dictating to the gooses the particulars of their goosehood.

496

Nothing is more devastating to women than disconnection; to men, disempowerment.

497

Men tend to be territorial, protecting what they own; women tend to be relational, protecting who they cherish.

498

For some 400 millennia, our kind has flourished thusly: The children circled around the hearth, looking no further than each other, being easily themselves; the women circled around the children, keeping a close watch, being easily themselves; the men circled at the perimeter, eyes cast outward, being easily themselves. Now what?

499

Biblically, Eve is the afterthought
Biologically, Adam is
Cosmologically, both are

500

What prattle is for women, pomp is for men.

501

Like all the other parts of us, the human voice was designed around purpose—basso for authority; treble for urgency.

502

Among women, there's an unwritten rule that no one will attempt to rise above the others—and God help her who tries. Among men, there's a tacit understanding that everyone will attempt to rise above the others—and God help him who's left behind.

503

For men, rules are the underpinning of all relationship; for women, relationship is the underpinning of all rules.

504

Women who fail with men seek the counsel of psychotherapists. Men who fail with women become psychotherapists.

505

Men spend money to demonstrate wealth; women, to demonstrate worth.

506

Boys tend to be adept at manipulating numbers and physical space; girls, at manipulating words and emotional space. Such is the practicality of complementarity.

507

The biggest difference between men and women over 30 is that most women of this age have left their childhood behind.

508

If girls can be tom-boys but boys can't be nancy-girls; if gals can be guys but guys can't be gals; if women can be one of the boys but men can't be one of the girls, where's the justice!

509

If the "weaker sex" can weep in public and apologize in private, but the stronger sex can do neither, what does it mean to be the "weaker sex?'

510

What does it say about our kind that we continue to allow women and girls to be mistreated by the very guardians whose sacred trust it is to protect them?

511

Women are perfectly suited to nurturing children; men, to producing them. Perfection indeed!

512

In assessing the power of culture to define the norms of gender, we might want to remind ourselves of which came first.

513

What men have wrought of concrete and steel has probably doomed the world beyond all possibility of redemption, save one—what women might yet weave of compassion and inclusion.

514

Make eye contact with a woman and be warmed with a smile; make eye contact with a man and be chilled with a stare

515

Females are gened to defer; males, to defy.

516

What latter-day Chanticleer is not late to discovering what the hens already know?

517

When women feel bad, they shop until they drop; when men feel bad, they drink until they drop.

518

Men own; women possess.

519

All women are mothers; not all men are fathers.

520

To be reminded of the majesty of complementarity, one need only bask in a duet.

521

We need more duets.

33
Mental Health

522

Self-care begins with holding one's symptoms in contempt.

523

When ill, do well things; when down, do up things; when blue, do red things. What we do, we become.

524

No craving feeds itself.

525

Self-regard comes from doing unto others as you would have them do unto you, even when they don't deserve it.

526

Psychotherapy flourishes because listening does not.

527

The best remedy for a dehydration of one's spirit is a hydration of one's brow.

528

Few are the days of gloom that cannot be brightened with one small success; shining a pair of shoes for the first time in a year is not too small a success.

529

There's a remedy for emotional constipation too, but it doesn't come in a bottle.

530

Much of what is peddled as Christianity would carry a warning from the Surgeon General under any other name.

531

There are two ways to fundamentally change ourselves—edit our genes, or amend our beliefs. The first option being impractical, the second improbable, it would seem we are pretty much stuck with who we are.

532

To know others we must first know ourselves. Or is it the other way round?

533

There are two ways to put people down—regale them with stories of your successes, or remind them of their failures. Just to be sure, you might want to do both.

534

A pill a day will keep your doctor's Jacuzzi at just about 85.40 F.

535

The tragedy of victimhood is not so much the original injury as it is the endless cycles of scabbing and picking that follow.

536

A neurotic is he who avoids going out for breakfast for fear of having to decide between sunny-side-up and over-easy.

537

The best way to lose weight is to feed the hunger, not the hankering.

538

In the absence of self-forgiveness, self-loathing is a life sentence.

34
Money & Wealth

539

If money can't buy happiness, why do so many of us complain about 1% of the population owning 50% of the wealth?

540

Why, after handling money, do our fingers feel so dirty?

541

Most of what glitters needs constantly to be re-plated.

542

The hundred dollar bill consists of four tenths of an ounce of paper and three tons of trust.

543

More than moolah we need meaning.

544

What is too easily got is too easily gone.

545

How many of us on our way to work, happening upon a suitcase filled with $100 bills, would complete the journey?

35
Music

546
Some prefer to compose, others to sing;
aren't they, though, the very same thing?

547
To sing is to soar
with the angels of lore.

548
Would we take life so lightly
had we to audition nightly?

549
Music is in the ear of the decoder.

550
Take "rap;" spell it backward;
tack it to the end of itself.
Who knew?

551
At least with music we always know what the score is.

552
Some birds trill, others tweet;
Some keep going, others repeat.

553
Music is a mystery, even to the Great Composer.

36
Nature

554
Mother Nature is no sentimentalist; what works, she retains; what does not, she abandons. Good luck t'yah.

555
Nature is conservative at the core, liberal around the perimeter.

556
All local symmetry is approximate; all cosmic symmetry, statistical.

557
From our perspective, cooperation and competition are opposites; from nature's, two faces on the same Eve.

558
Logic is the territory; math, the map.

559
Nature is the ultimate tinkerer, always tweaking here and there; never quite satisfied.

560
Mother Nature gives life, not love.

561
Mathematics is the language of the ideal, not of the real.

562
If gravity is a form of energy and energy is equivalent to mass, and mass has gravity, then gravity must have gravity, which must have gravity, which must have gravity . . .

563

Quantum mechanics tells us that reality exists in a physical state only when it's being observed; otherwise, it remains in a state of infinite possibility. So far, it is silent on whether or not one needs 20-20 vision in order to qualify as an observer.

564

String theory posits that reality is composed of one-dimensional objects having no physical substance vibrating in ten-dimensional space. So far, it's silent on how something having no substance can vibrate.

565

In the West, it's turtles all the way down;
in the East, serpents all the way 'round.

566

Nature loathes a straight line.

37
Nation & Society

567

Civilization is the sum total of the rebellion of the few against the conformity of the many.

568

Add up all the lies, misrepresentations, prevarications, bait-and-switches, and shameless dissemblings; sprinkle on a few jimmies, and whadaya got?

569

A nation of individuals is not the same thing as a nation.

570

The ultimate result of diversity is a nation of strangers.

571

When the divide is wide, separation is certain.

572

What compassion is to kindness, empathy is to civility.

573

Woe to any nation whose citizens come to believe their government owes them more than they owe each other.

574

Imperious, white-capped raptors to the contrary, the de facto symbol of the United States of America is the American ego.

575

When dodge ball and red ink are banned from our schools to forestall damaging the psyches of our tender children, what is likely to be the fate of the surprise quiz and the book report?

576

Some baptize arrogance and call it religion; others weave it into a flag and call it nation.

577

A nation prospers in spite of its government, not because of it.

578

The state of a nation is the state of its family.

579

America's new Big Three: Ignorance, Arrogance, and Incompetence.

580

Love binds a family; fear, a nation.

581

To reject one form of conformity is to embrace another.

582

Where there is ritual, there is continuity; where relationship, civility.

583

Woe to a nation of the unread.

584

We have become with our strip malls, big-box stores, and mega-schools an archipelago of alienation.

585

So goes the barn, so goes the farm.

38
Odds & Ends

586
Lend today; regret tomorrow.

587
For every promise kept, a hundred not.

588
Saying you're sorry is meaning it; apologizing, not so much

589
Dreams make perfect sense and then you wake up.

590
The greatest of treasures are hidden in plain sight.

591
Nobility, thy name is horse.

592
We fill our hearts with angst to the extent we empty our souls of meaning.

593
Blessed be the bullet that fits no chamber.

594
Diversity, like the May pole, would amount to little in the absence of a common core.

595
Slogans are tattoos writ in washable ink.

596
When brush stroke by brush stroke we paint ourselves as Helpless in the Face of Circumstance, there comes a time when Mover of Mountains becomes lost as a title.

597
Regret hath the greatest of company.

598

Risk contrition and few are the wrongs that will not be forgiven thee.

599

Innocence advertised is innocence lost.

600

It's worth being a curmudgeon just for the title.

601

Alchemy is much maligned, yet what noisome little itch cannot be transformed into pure joy merely by the scratching of it?

602

Pets are people minus the attitude.

603

Who we really are, we do not need to advertise; what we really are, we do not need to prove.

604

But for the gadflies among us, the earth would still be flat; disease would still be the doings of evil spirits; and the Emperor would still be parading around in his new clothes.

605

The gift that flatters is to the giver.

606

We can fake who we really are only until such time we must act without benefit of forethought.

607

Darkness cloaks evil for the meek,
mystery for the bold.

608

Giving a damn can pretty much ruin the day for those who don't.

609

There is community only to the extent there is concern.

610

We are masters of our fate to the extent we are masters of our beliefs.

611

Better stung by a bee than a hornet.

612

If two heads are better than one, what about three?

613

Believing it is ninety percent of becoming it.

614

It's impossible to be a caregiver and a care pretender at the same time. One has to choose.

39

Observations & Perspectives

615

Sticks and stones will break our bones; words, our spirit.

616

Everything has its cost;
air conditioning gained
is song of sparrow lost

617

What on Christmas Eve brightly burns, on Christmas Day fills four urns.

618

Regarding a noisome someone a mosquito makes him all the easier to swat.

619

I never met a textster who wasn't all thumbs.

620

Each moment we keep more than we require, we condemn a child somewhere in the world to an untimely death.

621

Absent contrast, naught.

622

A seed planted is not a harvest reaped.

623

A cloudburst is a ruined picnic one moment, a rainbow the next.

624

Worse forms of blindness there can be
than not being able to see.

625

Even the grave most visited is soon forgot.

626

Gaze upon a pond made agitated by the agitation around it, and be agitated. Peer upon a pond made quiet by the quietude around it, and be quieted

627

The ability to speak is a miracle; most of what is spoken is not.

628

What we see depends on the windows through which we peer.

629

Time was when, if a stranger smiled at us, we answered in kinds; today we reach for our wallet.

630

Landing is falling by any other name. Have a nice flight.

631

Sleep is for replenishing the body; solitude for replenishing the soul.

632

Perfection is a fair maiden forever imprisoned in the highest tower of the imagination.

633

It is through the eyes of others we see ourselves.

634

What possession does not possess?

635

'Tis not from the top of the smallest tree we can behold the forest.

636

To desire is to salivate; to yearn, investigate.

637

If the caterpillar were not slave to a higher crave,
would it find its way to wing?

638

There's a reason they put chlorine in public pools.

639

Whether a glass is half full or half empty depends on
whether the glass is being filled or emptied.

640

Context is everything.

641

The higher the mountain, the deeper the valley; the
deeper the valley, the higher the mountain.

642

Nothing is forever, except forever.

40
Poetry

643

Time was when the aim of the poet was art; today it's tenure.

644

To be read, be readable.

645

A ditty a day gives the poet a say.

646

The problem with poetry these days is you're never quite certain what's afoot.

647

One nice thing about poetry is that you can collect it either by the meter or by the bard.

648

Every parent's worst nightmare—finding a volume of poetry under their teenager's mattress.

649

What would happen if more poets than quarterbacks got asked for their autograph?

650

Robert Frost is still read today because he drew his metaphors from the earth, versus the ether.

651

A poet aspires to be published, an artist, collected.

652

To rhyme can be sublime, but often is not.

653

The modern poet tends to have absolutely nothing to say but to say it uncommonly well.

654

Novels chatter
Memoirs prattle
Essays drone
Exposés giggle
Romances purr
Poetry sings

655

Uncovering hidden meanings tends to be a lot easier if you hold a degree in forensic semantics.

656

What if Emily Dickinson had invited Walt Whitman to view her butterflies?

657

The pun is great fun, even when you can't think o' one

658

Verses that rhyme tend to be much convoluted;
verses that do not, little saluted.

659

A poem needs humility; the poet, even more.

660

If you've read a line five times and it still doesn't make sense, place the blame where it belongs.

661

The four species of poetry—transparent, translucent, opaque, utterly inscrutable.

41
Power

662
To the strong goes the growl; to the weak, the grovel.

663
All politicians who promise big changes should be asked to define their terms.

664
Power is rarely offered; one must at least put in a request.

665
Only those reluctant to power are to be trusted with it.

666
If a hierarchy is not imposed from above, one will emerge from below.

667
The only cure for metastasized ambition is a radical egoectomy.

668
Power hardens; absolute power calcifies.

669
We possess as much power over our lives as we have the courage to use.

670
We do not have the power to change who we fundamentally are; only the power to change what we daily do.

671
Only we the viewers have the power to restrain those who would violate any standard of behavior to win a higher rating.

672

Televising a major sporting event at 9:00 p.m. on a school night is a powerful message.

673

Where the desire to attain power is great, the desire to keep it will be even greater.

674

Those who seek power should never be trusted with it.

675

One way to attain power is to refuse it.

42
Quality

676
We do our best work when we regard what we do as who we are.

677
Quality is 95% skill and 5% attitude, except when it's 95% attitude and 5% skill.

678
When "Quality is job 1," it isn't.

679
The quality of a relationship is the quality of the two people in it.

680
Quality is its own reward.

681
In his quest for quality, the author of Zen and Art of Motorcycle Maintenance only needed to turn around and hug his passenger.

43
Race, Difference & Bigotry

682

Why is it we permitted to recognize differences in aptitude between breeds of Canis familiaris but not between races of Homo sapiens?

683

The issue is not whether there are differences between us, but whether those differences make any difference.

684

To preclude difference is to deny the true promise of diversity.

685

Relative worth is judgment; relative difference, acknowledgement.

686

You are the parent of a three-year-old girl badly injured in an auto accident. Your child needs to undergo brain surgery immediately or she will die. Three surgeons are available: one black, one brown, one white. You have no other information and three seconds to make a decision.

687

Behind every veil of political correctness is a moral coward.

688

Easy it is to denigrate from afar; not so easy face to face.

44
Rights & Responsibility

689

For every action, a reaction; for every right, a responsibility.

690

The right to vote implies the right not to; the right to live, the right not to; the right to aspire, the right not to. No coin of the realm can be all heads, no tails.

691

No greater responsibility hath any adult than to protect every child's right to an abiding innocence.

692

If Wal-Mart sold only responsibilities, would there still be a Black Friday?

693

The right to pursue happiness does not include texting while holding dominion over the fast lane.

694

There is no such thing as free speech. There is only responsible speech.

695

Why is it the rights of a pedestrian trump those of a driver until such time the former becomes the latter?

696

What right did Lincoln have to force the South into remaining in the union? Was it the same right George III had to force the colonies into remaining in the empire?

697

Entitlements bankrupt; absolute entitlements bankrupt until the end of time.

698

Every right is in relation to.

699

Metastasizing into almost every aspect of life today is a sense of entitlement to a level of comport it would be unthinkable to be denied.

700

We have the absolute right to ignore every social ill on the planet, and the absolute responsibility not to.

701

Rights are the arrow of our concern pointing inward; responsibilities, the arrow of our concern pointing outward.

702

The right to bear arms carries the responsibility to keep the chamber empty, the trigger locked, the owner sober.

703

If we count our rights but not our responsibilities, there can be no justice in the world; and if no justice, no trust; and if no trust, no cooperation; and if no cooperation, no civilization.

45
Science & Cosmology

704
All measurement is approximate; all boundary, illusion.

705
When the map is the territory, there is no territory.

706
The model is not the machine.

707
There are two kinds of windows through which we can peer into Nature's chamber of secrets; one is made of stained glass, the other is not.

708
Science is the art of giving up one theory for a better one.

709
Truth is a set of Chinese boxes. Science is the hand that opens each box to reveal the next.

710
Too few science books are read because too few are readable.

711
So powerful is our need for religion that we tend to make even science into one.

712
The progression of science is mostly a history of little Davids of truth winning an occasional battle against the Goliaths of entrenched belief.

713
Underlying all complexity is an elegant simplicity.

714

Revealed truth and empirical truth are not worlds apart; they are universes apart.

715

There is truth only where there is doubt.

716

The next time you feel diminished by the great minds of this world, consider this: No one knows what mass is, or what gravity is, or what space is, or what energy is. No one knows how the brain works or what consciousness is. No one knows where or how life began or how any of us gets from a single cell at conception to a fully formed organism at birth. In our exquisite dummyhood, we have the greatest of company.

717

Mathematical truth is a thin film of iridescence floating over a vast unfathomable depth.

718

Physics in not mathematical; it's phenomenal.

719

The universe contains all the information it requires to exist and not a syllable more.

720

Nothing in the universe can be isolated from everything else. Every piece is as if stuck in an elevator with every other piece.

721

Only nothing can be created out of nothing.

46
Sex & Marriage

722

'Tis a puzzle, this sex thing;
is it a blessing to please,
or a curse to sting?

723

The enduring marriage is not a careful accounting of plusses and minuses, but a spontaneous flow of gives and takes.

724

Nothing reveals our alienation from the lessons of the land more than the prevailing attitude that marriage can bear a bounty of fruit in the absence of any weeding or feeding.

725

As long as the media control our expectations, the fact of sex will never quite live up to the fantasy.

726

Nothing reveals our servitude to our biology more than our sexuality.

727

Which tribe likely had the higher survival rate; the one that enlisted homosexuals to protect the women and children while the mated males were absent, or the one that anticipated the phobias of today's Darwinian deniers?

728

Marriage is a duet in which each partner plays second fiddle to the other.

729

In courtship, we discover whether we love each other; in marriage, whether we like each other.

730

Marriage is like a tea rose; it's never without thorns and it only blooms if daily attended to.

731

If marriage is little more than barter—
as claimed by many much smarter –
how is it it makes us so much larger?

732

Marriage is turning the "m" in "me" upon its head.

733

Many a marriage goes flat the moment the fizz does.

734

A marriage is best built on common ground. Keeping separate isles requires not only the construction and maintenance of costly bridges, but also the time and effort to cross over them.

735

Sexual arousal is a form of madness for which no cure will ever be sought much less found.

736

Does one have sex as in the example of tea,
or does one do sex as in the case of lunch?

737

What if every marriage vow included a pledge to sacrifice one's life to save the other's?

47
Sports

738
To have a team is to have a tribe.

739
All spectator sports are participatory.

740
We need to take the money out of $port$ before sports takes the money out of u$.

741
One man's cricket match is another's cock fight.

742
When winning is "the only thing", everybody loses.

743
What might Caligula have done, do you think, if the Coliseum had tried to charge him $2,599 for a front-row seat?

744
Can we go back to choosing up sides?

48
Success & Failure

745

Those most likely to succeed are those who rely on the talents they have, not the ones they wish they had.

746

Confucius say, Man who work for self never complain about boss.

747

Success is to a sharpened blade what failure is to a dull one.

748

We are judged not by our failures, but by our attempts.

749

We would not be half so shamed by the great writers of the world had they left behind their first drafts.

750

The world loves best not those with the most talent, but those who make the most out of the talents they have.

751

It's not how our income stacks up that matters; it's how it stacks up against the other guy's.

752

Expediency is the quickest way to success, and the surest way to ruin.

753

'Tis not the victories won we reminisce, but the battles waged.

754

There are nobler ways of gaining notice in this world than by making the most noise.

755
It may never be too late, but the longer we wait the harder it's going to be.

756
It's always better to begin badly than not at all.

757
The key to solving any problem is taking the time to determine what the problem really is.

758
The secret to scaling a great height is to look no further ahead than the next handhold.

759
Having is nothing if we do not do with what we have; knowing is nothing if we do not do with what we know.

760
Many are called but few have the gumption to get there.

761
The greater the anticipation, the deeper the disappointment.

762
Most bad decisions are not the result of bad thinking but of good thinking applied to bad information.

763
To stop losing a fortune on college football, stop betting on your alma mater.

764
Before success can smile, discipline must frown.

765
Play not to win, but for the struggle; the sweat is the victory.

766
Pain is the price of prevailing.

767
There is no joy in safety; only comfort.

768

Why is it that those who keep boasting they can do it better tend to be the very ones who are always avoiding every opportunity to prove it?

769

The easy part is doing well what's worth doing; the hard part is determining what's worth doing.

770

Many launch rockets to lofty heights in their dreams; few awaken to find themselves aboard.

771

Pity those born into wealth, for they can never know the joy of earning one's own way.

772

Our net worth is not what we own minus what we owe, but what we have given away minus what we still retain.

773

What we talk ourselves into today we should talk ourselves out of tomorrow, first light.

774

We can only be as successful as we allow ourselves to feel.

775

There are as many keys to success as there are doors to open.

776

We are limited not by our abilities, but by our imagination.

777

Defeat is the way to self-confidence; failure, to self-pity.

49
Technology

778
What's feasible is not necessarily what's practical.

779
Technology can make us more productive; it cannot make us better company.

780
Users of machines tend to become them.

781
The feel of steel is not the scent of wood.

782
Technology can mend a heart; it cannot stitch a soul.

783
Technology can give us means; it cannot give us purpose.

50
This & That

784

The second greatest invention of all time is the Mute button.

785

Is a pun declared unintended still unintended?

786

What we do is forever won; what we do not do, forever lost.

787

An aphorism is a little block of truth chiseled and polished into a comely little kewpie.

788

To pursue the sweet is to risk the sour.

789

Anticipation is nine-tenths the pleasure.

790

What dream is not an allegory; what allegory, not a dream?

791

A chore poorly performed is little sooner a monkey off one's back than a nettle on one's conscience.

792

Once upon a time, there were two kinds of storytellers— the enthraller, for whom the story was the thing, and the philosopher, for whom the moral was the thing.

793

The only true gift is anonymous.

794

We weren't made for big. Big is disconnection, anonymity, diminishment, alienation, marginalization, inefficiency, miscommunication, and a hundred other little miseries. We were made for small.

795

If it is demeaning to flatter our way into the good graces of an earthly prince, what is it to bow and scrape our way into the good graces of a heavenly prince?

796

Trees are not the only things that don't grow very well in asphalt.

797

Own not, owe not.

798

Why is it no big deal for a bar-mitzvah to be held in a YMCA, all but impossible for a confirmation to be held in a temple?

799

Summer ain't over 'til the last rose blooms.

800

To get what you need, let go of what you want.

801

If a self-help regimen promises you it won't hurt, won't make you sweat, and won't take more than five minutes a day, fuhgetaboutit.

802

No one can be so exceptional as to be exempt from sacrificing something of himself for the sake of others.

803

To focus the meaning, axe all the adverbs.

804

Slumber is the filling between layers of living.

51
Truth

805
Truth is like a house cat; it purrs in our presence but never comes when called.

806
To abide a lie is to become one.

807
To quench our deepest thirst, we need only drink of the wellspring within.

808
We tend to see firstly what we want to see; secondly what we expect to see; thirdly what others would have us see. Only rarely do we see what's actually there.

809
A marketplace for truth would truly be bizarre.

810
We reveal the truth of ourselves far more with our eyes than with our tongue.

811
Truth tends to be more tease than please.

812
Truth is what happens when fear forgets to set the alarm.

813
Some seek truth by compass, others by map;
some simply close their eyes, and take a nap.

814
Only the naked truth and bare-bottomed babes know no shame.

815

Common sense is like a pigeon in a park; we all see it, but few of us take any notice.

816

All essential truth is writ large and back lit.

817

Memory is more novelist than librarian.
Truth surrenders only to the flag of the indefatigable.

818

Truth is like a tanager in an orchard; we can catch glimpses of it now and then, but rarely the whole of it.

819

Moral truth is neither absolute nor relative; it is both.

820

The Tooth Fairy is a lie; the Easter Bunny is a lie; Santa Claus is a lie; the Devil is a lie; every ad ever aired on television is a lie; most of what every politician has ever said is a lie. No wonder only "In God We Trust."

821

There are only three ways to truth—by faith (scripture), by experience (wisdom), by inquiry (science).

822

If there is an all-powerful god, there can be no perpetrator of calamity but him.

52
Unsolicited Advice

823

To get to where you want to go, get going.
To get to where you need to go, wait a second.

824

If there's no light at the end of the tunnel, you're in the wrong tunnel.

825

Advice from my barber: Never kiss anybody's ass. Make 'em all think you might, but never actually do it.

826

If it's got more than three knobs or buttons, and one of those is the On/Off switch, don't buy it!

827

If you tend to be a noun, try spending part of each day being a verb.

828

Choose your companions carefully; who they are you will be.

829

Judge your level of success not against what you see in your neighbor's driveway but against what you see in his eyes.

830

Regard every stranger you meet as the Buddha just back from basking under the Bodhi tree.

831

Beware not of the strong but of the weak; it's not the strong whose footsteps you hear behind you.

832

If your life feels out of balance, instead of shifting the load, try moving the fulcrum.

833

Beware of anything that begins with a flash and ends with a bang.

834

Advice from Bill Shakespeare: If you can't think of the perfect word, make up one.

835

Never vote for anyone named Bubba or cast a ballot for anyone named Rupert.

836

When all else fails, consult a 12-year-old.

837

If you're going to take the road less traveled, be sure to pack a lunch.

838

Better to be not in the wrong than ever in the right.

53
Vanity, Narcissism & Greed

839

Vanity is trying to make the maple of us look like the mahogany of them.

840

So expensive is vanity these days that only the vain can afford it.

841

Vanity is spending three hours in a tanning booth the day before returning home from a vacation.

842

Narcissism is rehearsing your opinion while pretending to be listening to someone else's.

843

"Me and you" reflects one reality; "you and I," another.

844

Greed is good or bad depending on who we're talking about.

845

Is lusting after eternal life any different from lusting after thy neighbor's wife?

54
Violence

846
No sooner is a man to violence than at the heels of humiliation.

847
As insult begets insult, so blow begets blow.

848
A man at peace with himself is not at war with others.

849
Every act of violence is a flood that could have been prevented by constructing the dam lower, not higher.

850
Delay justice, risk retribution.

851
Violence bears fruit of two kinds—damage beyond reparation, regret beyond remedy.

55
Wisdom

852

Wisdom begins when we realize no one in the wrong is not partly in the right; no one in the right is not partly in the wrong.

853

Wisdom is our reward for suffering through all those painful lessons we were always trying to avoid.

854

The road to wisdom is unpaved, unmarked, unlit, and the potholes only get larger.

855

We can have a wisdom tooth or a wise ass, but that seems to be pretty much it.

856

What if everything we put in our mouth had to pass a litmus test, and everybody we put in office had to pass a wisdom test?

857

Data is not information, information not knowledge, knowledge not wisdom.

858

To the clever goes complexity; to the wise, tranquility.

859

Can one be both wise and wily or does one have to choose?

860

If it takes sixty-four years for a medicine man to amass wisdom enough to lead a tribe, how many years should it take for someone to amass wisdom enough to lead a nation?

56
Women

861

What women lack in physical strength they more than make up for in adaptability.

862

First women were allowed to vote, then they were allowed to drive, then they were allowed to serve on juries, then they were allowed to work outside the home, then they were allowed to major in physics, then they were allowed to hold office, then they were allowed to serve in the infantry, and now, finally, they are allowed to "lean in."

863

Nature abides women to live longer than men because women are naturally inclined to give more than they take.

864

Women were designed to seek not power but the powerful.

865

Femininity is shaped by fashion but determined elsewhere. Culture can mold the clay; it cannot invent it.

866

When a man has something to say, he writes a book and goes on tour. When a woman has something to say, she calls a friend or hosts a tea.

867

We need more teas.

868

Why is there no Hall of Fame for church ladies?

869

Every man wants a son but needs a daughter

57
Work & Career

870
If empty work produces only more emptiness, what are we to fill ourselves with?

871
Why do we have to choose between "Business or pleasure?"

872
Careerism is the division of labor on steroids.

873
The emptier the work, the more frequent the snacks.

874
We are fortunate to the extent our talents and abilities translate into something the marketplace rewards; wise to the extent we pay no attention.

875
Career is mine eyes on me; contribution, mine eyes on thee.

876
Work that does not feed the soul kills it.

877
Career is turning from family and the nurturance of it toward self and the furtherance of it.

878
Careerism is meism with an iPad.

879
When feminism became careerism, Friedan became Faust.

880
More important than the food we eat is the job we keep.

Buns & Biscuits

1
Panel of Our Peers

OUR SYSTEM OF JUSTICE IS BASED ON THE THEORY THAT WE HAVE a fundamental right to be judged by a panel of our peers versus by the king's (or state's) representatives. To field a panel of our peers, we use random selection (conscription). (Once upon a time, we employed this same device to field an army of citizen-soldiers.)

What if our system of governance were similarly based? What if, at all levels, our personal and collective interests were represented not by self-interested, eminently-corruptible politicians, always seeking personal advantage, but by average citizens selected by lot?

What if there were no career politicians? No negative campaign ads? No endless electioneering? No gerrymandering. No entrenched partisanship. No shameless dissembling? No political robo-calls? No PACs? No pundits? No Donald Trumps?

What if our entire culture were constructed around the notion that every citizen, however humble in his or her abilities or achievements, was subject to conscription into public service, just as every (male) citizen was, once upon a time, was subject to conscription into a common defense? Indeed, isn't this what a democracy *really* is?

2

To Comply or Not to Comply

H OW MANY TIMES HAVE YOU HEARD SOMEONE SAY, OR HAVE
yourself said, "I had no choice?" In fact, there's *always* a choice,
is there not, even when the alternative is so distasteful we are
naturally inclined toward denying it even exists?

Take for example the situation of Sophie Zawistowska in William
Styron's *Sophie's Choice.* When Sophie is (literally) dragged off to
Auschwitz for having smuggled a ham to her dying mother, a sadistic
Nazi doctor tells her that one of her two children must die, apparently
in atonement for Sophie's grievous infraction. The doctor tells Sophie
also that she must choose which one of her children will be sacrificed,
which will be spared. Horrified, but seeing herself as having no choice,
Sophie chooses to sacrifice her daughter.

In fact, Sophie had a clear choice—*not* between siblings, but between
whether to comply with the doctor's demand or not to comply. The
latter option, not complying, might well have resulted in the death of
both children, as well as Sophie herself, but all three were as good as
dead anyway.

In the face of coercion—of any kind, from any source—it would
seem we always have at least one choice, between complying and not
complying.

But which to do?

If Sophie had chosen *not* to comply with what was being demanded of
her—had in other words told the sadistic doctor to take a hike—Styron's
novel would certainly have been a lot shorter, but would it not have been
a lot more powerful?

3

Power to the People!

W E AMERICANS TEND TO REGARD OUR "DEMOCRACY" AS BEING superior to every other form of governance on the planet. Unfortunately, our "democracy" is not really a democracy at all; it's a republic. We do not gather at the town hall every morning to vote on the issues of the day (although we used to do something similar to this, in New England at least, back in the day.) Instead, we elect surrogates to represent our interests at the town hall, and other surrogates to represent our interests at the county seat, and still other surrogates to represent our interests at the state house, and so on and so on.

The Founding Fathers chose to establish a representative form of government rather than a true democracy because democracies do not scale very well. It's one thing to cram a hundred local citizens into a town hall; quite another to cram a thousand, or ten thousand, or three-hundred million citizens, drawn from disparate communities, into anything resembling a town hall.

For many of us, though, whether we vote directly on the issues of the day, as in the case of a true democracy, or by way of surrogates, as in the case of a republic, is a mere technicality. In either case, we, the voters, hold ultimate power. In the case of a republic, if we don't like how our surrogates are voting on the issues of the day, we can replace them from the ranks of any number of alternative sources. For instance, we might elect hardcore ideologues from a fringe party, or zany zealots from the religious right, or overeducated elitists from the godless left, or greed-is-good fat cats from Wall Street, or billionaire robber barons from Big Business, or mindless meatheads from organized labor, or even bona fide boneheads from the sociopolitical fringe.

Or—if it weren't for the fact we were just too darn busy—we could even replace them with ourselves!

What a country!

4

Ms. Smith Goes to Philadelphia

I N INSTITUTING A REPRESENTATIVE FORM OF GOVERNMENT, THE Founding Fathers envisioned that the men (no women, heaven forbid) elected to represent the interests of average citizens would themselves be average citizens—artisans, tradesmen, merchants, farmers, roustabouts, clergymen, laborers—even lawyers!

They did not anticipate the emergence of a ruling class of professional legislators who would make a career out of running for, holding, and exploiting elected office, not to mention soliciting various "philanthropists" and "charitable interests" for millions upon millions of dollars with which to wage (so to say) relentlessly recurring political campaigns. Nor did they anticipate the bifurcation of the electorate into two opposing camps of closed-minded ideologues, strikingly resembling, in their obtuseness, Dr. Seuss's South-Going Zaxs and North-Going Zaxs. In other words, the Founding Fathers did not anticipate at least two principal ways in which the system of governance they had so carefully wrought could be corrupted and/or rendered ineffectual.

When a Magic Slate becomes too blackened or smudged to be serviceable, we pull up the cellophane and start over. Might it be time to do the same with our smudged and blackened republic? Might it be time indeed to first "kill all the politicians," and then send Ms. Smith to Philadelphia?

5
Are There No ERs?

s Ebenezer Scrooge discovered, by way of three nocturnal visitors, the soul of a man is revealed by how he treats the troubled and afflicted of the world. Likewise, by logical extension, is the soul of a nation revealed.

What are we to make of a nation, then, that assures access to quality health care to its In's (those In a job) but not to its Out's (those Out of a job)?

Does the availability and quality of health care have only a practical dimension, or is there also, or instead, a moral dimension?

How might Mr. Scrooge have answered this question *before* being visited by the mystical handiwork of three undigested pieces of potato?

How about *after* being visited?

6
The Last Tree

SOMEONE CUT DOWN THE LAST TREE ON EASTER ISLAND AND thereby sealed the fate of humankind on that island for all time.

Between 1970 and 2010, the world lost 52% of the 10,000 species of vertebrates that then existed. That's a permanent loss of 5,200 species in just 40 years.

In 1890, there were 1.2 million lions in the wild. Today there are 20,000. How long might it be, do you think, before someone shoots the last one?

7

Plato's Dream

I N *Republic*, PLATO IDENTIFIES FOUR FUNDAMENTAL FORMS OF governance and, by revealing the flaws inherent to each one, dismisses the ability of each one to ensure justice, which, for Plato, was the *raison d'être* of all governance. With no other form of governance available to ensure justice, Plato invented one—the benevolent dictatorship.

Essentially, Plato envisioned a ruling class that would be made up entirely of "philosopher-kings", men (no women, heaven forbid) who would be rendered incorruptible by being enlightened beyond all possibility of ever coming to value personal interest over the public good.

We can easily dismiss Plato's scheme as a quaint exercise in naïveté, until we are reminded that the human family has always been (by genetic imperative, it would seem) a de facto benevolent dictatorship, with one parent (usually the father) serving in the role of beneficent autocrat (father knows best). One could argue, in fact, that the human family could not have, as an institution, survived over the eons under any other form of governance.

Given this success story, might it be possible to scale it up such as to realize Plato's dream in the large? Might it be possible indeed to create a caste of incorruptible philosopher-kings to ensure justice for every human being, young or old, big or little, rich or poor, male or female?

Why are you laughing?

8
Trinity

SIMILAR TO CAESAR'S GAUL, AND CATHOLICISM'S GODHEAD, THE human psyche would appear to be divided into three parts, with each part being separate from the others in one sense, inextricably commingled in another. For the sake of argument, let's label these separate but inseparable parts the ego self, the soul self, and the agency self—collectively, the trinity of the self.

Under this scheme, the ego self is the survival self, the grand acquisitor. Its primary concern is satisfying the appetites and desires associated with basic needs. It is fear-driven, material-centered, and self-focused (i.e., the arrow of concern points ever inward). It seeks pleasure and avoids, or attempts to mitigate as much as possible, physical and psychic pain. Its primary goals are security, growth, preeminence, and propagation. Among the means to the ends of the ego self are food, money, power, status, success, sex, stuff—anything and everything that in some way represents survival and/or self-extension (mine over thine!).

The soul self is the social self, the grand contributor. Its primary concern is contributing to the well-being of the group, the tribe, the community—any and all others. The soul self is love-driven, meaning-centered, and other-focused (i.e., the arrow of concern points ever outward). It seeks fulfillment and avoids, or attempts to mitigate as much as possible, emptiness and despair. Its primary goals are enlightenment, meaning, wholeness, and harmony. Among the means to the ends of the soul self are truth, intimacy, authenticity, commitment, sacrifice, compassion, and collaboration.

The agency self is the judge, the mediator, the grand controller—or what we have come to call "free will." The agency self reasons, weighs evidence, agonizes, makes decisions. When Hamlet vacillates, "To be or not to be," it is Hamlet's agency self who is deliberating. If we choose preeminently to seek pleasure in our lives, it is our agency self who decides this (either directly or by abdicating control to the ego self). If we choose to balance the desires of the ego self against the yearnings of the soul self, it is likewise our agency self who decides this.

Given the current state of America, not to mention Gaul and the Catholic Church, which part of the trinity of the self would appear to be in charge? Toward what end eventually?

9
The End of Empathy

Y OU KNOW THE END OF EMPATHY IS AT HAND WHEN . . .

- There still aren't half enough stalls in the Women's Room.

- The young lady sitting behind you in the "quiet car" takes a call on her cell phone.

- Nothing announced on a PA system in a bus or subway car is intelligible.

- The instructions consist of a couple of indecipherable pictograms.

- Phone trees do not have an option for your need or issue.

- Catalog order clerks take your credit-card information before checking to see if the item you want to order is in stock.

- Drivers talking on their cell phone make no effort to move into the slow lane.

- The people sitting behind you in a movie theatre crackle candy wrappers throughout the show.

- No one apologizes for making you wait.

- No one apologizes period.

- "Newspaper delivery" is an oxymoron.

- Most items sealed in plastic bubbles can only be opened with the Jaws of Life.

- Drivers moving into the flow of traffic from an on-ramp force you into either sideswiping them or being rear-ended.

- The ER check-in clerk takes your insurance information before noticing that your eyes are fixed and dilated.

- Half the text on any given Web site is either too small or too washed out to be read.

- Every other Netflix DVD you receive in the mail is damaged.

- Men use toilets as urinals without raising the seat.

- The button holes on your shirts are too small for the buttons.

- Twenty percent of American children are allowed to go undernourished.

- You can no longer find a quiet place in any waiting room.

- No one can hear the airline captain's announcement above the engine noise.

- Street signs are either missing or too small to be read in time.

- Automatic toilets flush just before you sit down on the seat doily.

- You have to take your car to the dealer every spring and fall to have the clock reset.

10
On Courtship

OURTSHIP IS A DEVICE BY WHICH PHYSICAL AND EMOTIONAL entanglement can be incremented so that prospective mates for life can determine if they really want to commit "until death do us part." In short, courtship is a societal attempt to prevent costly mistakes that could have a negative impact on society at large. In our time, such costs include single-motherhood and all the ramifications that pertain thereto, as well as fatherless children and all the ramifications that pertain thereto.

In the past, courtship recognized the value of female virginity and, in fact, focused on preserving it. If a young woman lost her virginity outside wedlock, whether consensually or otherwise, she was deemed "ruined" (the same term used for financial bankruptcy). To understand the reason for this, we need to don our Darwinian bonnets.

The pre-human counterparts to the human female and human male had between them very different strategies for passing on their genes. The pre-human female was contrived by natural selection to have a small number of offspring, as reflected by the relatively small number of eggs she produced, and to invest a great deal of time and energy in nurturing her few offspring to reproductive age. The pre-human male, on the other hand, was contrived to have a large number of offspring, as reflected by the relatively large number of sperm he produced, and to invest little time or energy in nurturing his offspring to reproductive age.

As our forebears evolved into humans, and the maturation period for offspring greatly increased, it became necessary for both parents to invest a relatively large amount of time and energy in protecting and nurturing their mutual offspring. In order for this strategy to work, however, mating had to be for life, and therefore males had to be assured that their mate's offspring would be theirs and not someone else's. To accomplish this, nature invented the hymen, and human culture invented courtship.

Given the state of courtship in our time—the almost total loss of its original purpose—it is problematic whether mating for life (or even to the end of child-rearing) can long survive. Indeed, when we look at our culture today, what do we see in this regard?

What do we not see?

11
Father's Day

DESPITE A GENERAL DOWNGRADING OF THE VENERABLE INSTITUTION of motherhood, and a near-simultaneous general upgrading of "careerism" and "leaning in," one can still readily make a case for a genuinely honorific Mothers Day. Indeed, what we call "mother love"—the only species of love that is truly unconditional—still flourishes in the bosom of most mothers.

It has become increasingly difficult, however, to make a case for a genuinely honorific Fathers Day. The problem was captured in the example of Barack Obama, who chose to run for the U.S. presidency when his two daughters, Malia and Sasha, were only eight and five years old, respectively.

As in the case of John F. Kennedy (and several other young presidents), it was prima facie more important to Mr. Obama that he become President of the United States (the first <u>Black</u> President, one has to suspect) than it was for him to ensure that his daughters would enjoy a normal childhood characterized by normal relations with both parents.

This is not to judge Mr. Obama (or any of the other young presidents who made essentially the same choice), but to make a point about the general state of fatherhood in our time; namely, that fathers today seem to be ever more captive to personal ambition, to the general detriment of their families, most especially their children. Instead of being focused on the essential work of providing, guiding, and mentoring their offspring, fathers today seem almost compelled (likely by genetic as well as cultural imperatives) to pursue their personal "happiness" outside the bounds of hearth and home.

One has to wonder what might have happened to Holden Caulfield (the cynical protagonist in J.D. Salinger's *Catcher in the Rye*) had his high-powered lawyer-father been more active in his troubled son's life, especially after the death of Holden's beloved brother Allie. One similarly has to wonder what might have happened had Mr. Obama written a book about a half-Black/half-White father who had had the audacity to sacrifice his personal ambition for the general good and well-being of his family, not to mention, by way of example, for the general good and well-being of countless other families.

12
Finding Kanzus

NOT ONLY CAN'T JOHNNY READ; IT TURNS OUT HE CAN'T WRITE, spell, punctuate, cipher, think, infer, or find Kanzus on a map, either.

How did this happen?

Let us count the ways:

1. Johnny was forged in a culture in which learning for learning's sake, knowing for knowing's sake, understanding or for understanding's sake, has little intrinsic value.

2. Johnny was forged in a culture in which a majority of parents do not read to their children, do not take them to museums, and do not discuss the issues of the day with them.

3. Johnny was forged in a culture in which the average child spends over six hours a day, seven days a week, texting, friending, liking, cellphoning, apping, and instagramming.

4. Johnny was forged in a culture in which most MLB pitchers make more money per pitch, *per pitch*, than most teachers make in an entire school year.

5. Johnny was forged in a culture in which creationism is believed by sixty-two percent of the adult population to be an appropriate topic for study in public schools.

6. Johnny was forged in a culture in which any student who openly shows a passion for learning risks being teased and bullied, not to mention physically harmed.

7. Johnny was forged in a culture in which no one under sixty has any idea who Frank Baum is.

13

Papal Bull

W HEN I WAS A PINT, *the* CHURCH TOLD ME THAT MASTURBATION was an abomination (except, apparently, for those countless heathens who preceded Catholicism and therefore never received "God's holy word"). The logic behind this stance, I was told, was that spilling one's seed other than in the proper receptacle, under the proper conditions, was prima facie against "God's will." God invented sex, you see, not for loving couples to join with and pleasure each other, but for God-fearing couples to produce as many new little Catholics as possible.

Curiously unmentioned by *the* Church regarding the inherent evil (disorder) of masturbation, was the fact that masturbation for females did not involve spilling one's seed, and therefore could not warrant the same moral condemnation it did for boys. Indeed, it seemed to me that girls got to pleasure themselves with impunity while boys got to choose between chronic sexual frustration and being cast into a pit of hellfire for all eternity, in company, unavoidably, with mass murderers and serial rapists.

The Church also told me that "impure thoughts" were an abomination. An impure thought was any mental image visited upon or conjured by one's imagination that had anything to do with sex. The logic here presumably was that any mental image involving sex was prima facie one and the same with the act itself. Given this "logic," one had to wonder what God-fearing parent would risk providing her pubescent child with sex education, of any sort, for fear it might trigger an uncontrollable cascade of impure thoughts and thereby condemn her precious child to an unimaginable fate.

Child abuse comes in many forms, does it not?

14
American Exceptionalism

For America to declare herself "exceptional" is a lot like the Catholic Church declaring the pope infallible. The arrogance in both cases has the same rank odor, and even if it were true that a particular nation or culture was in fact "exceptional," merely declaring itself so would, in fact, be tantamount to confessing the opposite.

Remember Ford's "Quality is Job 1?" Was it?

Remember Allstate's "You're in Good Hands?" Were we?

Remember Burger King's "Have It Your Way?" Did we?

Remember Lockheed Martin's "We Never Forget Who We're Working For?" Did they?

It's tempting to invoke here, as the poster child of Exceptionalism, a certain supremacist / jingoist / ultra-nationalist, with a little buzz of a mustache, who, over a period of just six years, 1939 to 1945, in attempting to prove the supremacy of a certain mythical "master race," was responsible for the direct or indirect deaths of seventy million men, women, and children, including over four millions of his own exceptional people.

America first!

Numero Uno!

Love it or leave it!

15
Zero Sum

FOR ABOUT 400,000 YEARS, OUR FOREBEARS HAD LITTLE SENSE of "progress." Each succeeding generation largely mirrored the previous generation in experience, knowledge, technology, lifespan, and culture. Not only was there little or no change; there was little or no expectation of change.

Then something highly disruptive happened. Someone planted a seed, it sprouted, and almost overnight people were living longer, inventing new technologies, acquiring new knowledge, telling new stories (and writing them down), and aspiring toward "better" lives, not only for themselves, but for their children and grandchildren as well. "Progress," the notion of realizing a net gain over time, had taken root in the human psyche—where it has been deceiving us, generation after generation, ever sense.

Deceiving us?

It's right there in Newton's Third Law: For every action, there is an equal and opposite reaction. Zero sum. In the case of progress, for every gain, there has to be a commensurate loss. Take, for example, the eReader. For very gain realized by this device (mass storage, for example), there is a commensurate loss (the esthetic experience of the printed book, for example, not to mention the heady fragrance of bindery glue). If we were to sum up all such gains and losses relative to the use of the eReader, the net gain would effectively be zero.

The same is true of air conditioning (song of sparrow lost), famine relief (overpopulation), the leaf blower (loss of neighborhood tranquility), and so on and so on.

In the case of a shotgun blast, we see (and feel) the zero-summing elements—action and reaction—both immediately and clearly. In the case of a new technology, however, or an improved methodology, we do not always see (or feel), immediately or clearly, the losses associated with the gains. We must at least look for them.

16

The Circle
Is the Only Geometry

ONSIDER THE NOTION OF A UNIVERSE THAT BEGINS WITH A BIG Bang (First Cause) and expands ever afterward, in linear fashion, toward infinity. Can such a universe truly expand forever (in other words, can space "stretch" an infinite amount), or must it eventually collapse, in the manner of an overextended rubber band?

The famous yin-yang symbol, spawned of Eastern philosophy thousands of years ago, would appear to suggest an answer.

The first thing we notice about this ancient symbol is its fundamental cyclicality. The second thing we notice is its fundamental duality. What we notice specifically is a pair of complementary opposites (suggesting fetuses) locked in a beginning-less, endless cycle of mutual creation, whereby each complement simultaneously defines the other by making the other necessary. There must be existence, for example (as represented by the white fetus), because there is nonexistence (as represented by the black fetus), and vice versa. There must be a set of negative real numbers because there is a set of positive real numbers, and vice versa. There must be a notion of up because there is a notion of down, and vice versa. There must be yin because there is yang, and vice versa—ad infinitum.

There is no First Cause here, or linear progression ad infinitum, or endlessly stretching space. In short, the circle is the only geometry.

17
The Limits of Complexity

HUMAN BEINGS EVOLVED IN A CONTEXT OF RELATIVE SIMPLICITY. To be sure, life was forever a challenge for our distant forebears—one could as easily be a meal as in pursuit of one—but it was not frenzied or fragmented. One was readily able to focus one's attention in a single direction toward realizing a single goal. One could expect, therefore, to seldom, if ever, suffer from such emergent disorders as existential angst, chronic fatigue, anxiety attacks, neuroses, chronic insomnia, identity crises, panic attacks, clinical depression, or psychic burnout.

Not so in today's world, in which most of us have more in common with the hare in *Alice in Wonderland* than we might care to admit. Alas—

I'm late, I'm late for
A very important date.
No time to say hello, good-bye,
I'm late, I'm late, I'm late

If we were to plot the amount of complexity intruding into our lives over time, we would likely come up with a curve bending ever more steeply upward toward infinity. Of course, we could never cope with infinite complexity, or anything approaching it, but just how much complexity *can* we cope with?

How many more "user friendly" devices can we cope with; how much more "multitasking" can we cope with; how many more "simplified" tax forms can we cope with; how many more "your call is important to us" phone trees can we cope with; how much more "Paperwork Reduction Act" bureaucracy can we cope with; how much more cross-product incompatibility can we cope with; how many more unsolicited interruptions can we cope with; how much more "having it all" can we cope with before the entire out-of-balance enterprise comes crashing down around us and upon us?

Do you get a sense we are about to find out?

18
Ode to Real Books

REAL BOOKS, TACTILE BOOKS, ARE NOT JUST PAPER-AND-CLOTH artifacts. They are old friends, constant companions, intimate snuggle-buddies. They are part of the "village" of noble characters that helped form and shape us. They are pleasing to the touch; to the eye; and, yes, even to the nose. They are part of the wallpaper with which we decorate the various compartments of our soul. They speak to us, they comfort us. As in the case of their owners, they take on ever more character with age. They are works of art. They grace our shelves and reveal by association at least part of who we are. They are food for thought. They are keepsakes, they are heirlooms. They conjure sweet moments of youthful thrall. Real books, flesh-and-blood books, are what keep the day separated from the night.

19
Jerks, Jesters & Jackals

GENERALLY SPEAKING, HUMAN FEMALES ARE BORN ANGELIC AND must be made devilish; while human males are born devilish and must be made angelic. This is an oversimplification, of course, but it points to a fundamental truth about our kind: If human males are to become beneficent members of society, if they are to become true gentle-men, they must be transformed from what Nature would have them be to what civil society needs them to be.

In times past, every tribe of humans on the planet devised and employed a formal ritual, a rite of passage, for transforming its pull-the-wings-off-butterflies boys into ready-to-sacrifice-all-for-the-greater-good men. (In our world, only a few such rituals remain, the Vision Quest being one, the Bar Mitzvah being another.)

Central to these rites of passage was the ordeal. Each candidate for manhood had to endure some kind of physical and / or psychic challenge as a way of earning his way into official manhood. Most of these challenges involved measured inflictions of fear, pain, and / or deprivation. The boys who were able to endure their ordeal, who were "man enough," were blessed into the community of men.

Not so the unblessed of today. Needing to be men, sometimes desperately so, but having no official rituals by which to render them such, boys today tend to make up their own rites of passage—"scoring", for example, or bullying, or street-fighting, or binge-drinking, or drag-racing, or body-tattooing, or drugging, or dropping-out, or road-raging, or desecrating, or vandalizing—or simply being insufferable cads at every opportunity. The ultimate result—instead of a brotherhood of responsible, contributing members of the community at large—has been, and continues to be, and likely will continue to be ad infinitum, an "animal house" filled with jerks, jesters, and jackals.

20
A Few Questions for You

WHEN THE SPARTANS OF ANCIENT GREECE ENGAGED AN ENEMY on the battlefield, it was always the Spartan king who would lead the charge. Question: Can you name any "king" today who would similarly put himself in harm's way?

The day before he was assassinated, Martin Luther King Junior said this at a public rally: "Like anybody, I would like to live a long life. Longevity has its place. But I'm not concerned about that now. I just want to do God's will. And He's allowed me to go up to the mountain. And I've looked over. And I've seen the Promised Land. I may not get there with you. But I want you to know tonight, that we, as a people, will get to the Promised Land. And I'm happy, tonight. I'm not worried about anything. I'm not fearing any man."

QUESTION: Are there indications of true leadership here? If so, what are they?

In 1962, Nelson Mandela of South Africa was sentenced to life in prison for engaging in anti-apartheid activities. Freed from prison after twenty-seven years, Mr. Mandela fostered the negotiations with the white establishment that would ultimately lead to a multiracial democracy. As president of South Africa, Mr. Mandela sought reconciliation rather than retribution, and pursued policies aimed at combating poverty and inequality for all.

QUESTION: Are there indications of true leadership here? If so, what are they?

21

Expediency! Expediency! Expediency!

E XPEDIENCY IS THE QUALITY OR STATE OF ATTAINING OR ATTEMPTING to attain a desired end by readiest means. Acts of expediency are amoral at best and shamelessly unprincipled at worst. There is ever about them a Machiavellian odor.

A politician plants a false rumor about his opponent in order to impugn his opponent's reputation. The politician justifies his act of expediency with the rationalization that he is by far the better candidate but the voters are too stupid to see it.

Trained interrogators torture prisoners of questionable culpability as a way of extracting information the prisoners might or might not possess. The interrogators justify their act of expediency with the rationalization that should there be another 9/11 attack they don't want to be held in any way culpable.

The Catholic Church transfers a pedophile from one diocese to another in order to shield his egregious breeches of trust from public exposure. The Church justifies its act of expediency with the rationalization that the Church's reputation is far more important than the innocence and spiritual well-being of a few expendable children.

An 18th-century statesman writes a false account of a massacre of colonial women and children by "savages" allied with the British. He justifies his act of expediency with the rationalization that the most efficient way of transforming a potential threat into a target for elimination is by demonizing it.

A publisher charges $29.95 for a book instead of $30.00 as a time-proven way of tricking the brain of potential buyers into seeing "20" instead of "30". What the hell—everybody's doing it!

22
What If Only Women Could Vote?

BEFORE THE ARRIVAL OF THE WHITE MAN IN NORTH AMERICA, the Wyandot Indians comprised twelve clans, with each clan being governed by a clan council, and each council being presided over by a clan chief.

Each of the twelve councils consisted of at least five persons—one man, and <u>only</u> one man, and at least four women. (There was no limit on the number of women.) The council women regulated the affairs of the clan and selected the clan chief. In other words, only the women of the Wyandot could vote.

As is well established by now, human males have, in general, pretty much been in charge over the past 200 millennia, and have pretty much screwed everything up.

The legacy is legion—amassing and misusing personal power, carrying greed to ever new heights, disenfranchising and marginalizing women, waging endless war, imagining ever-more-lethal weapons for waging ever-more endless war, killing off entire species, inventing homophobic and misogynist religions, carrying on "blood feuds," allowing millions of children to perish of starvation and preventable disease, normalizing rape, degrading the environment, begetting then abandoning legions of "fatherless" children—and that's just for starters!

The underlying problem here, given the consistency of this sad legacy, not to mention its enormity, would seem to be inherent to the Y chromosome, which, although puny in physical size relative to its Queen Bee counterpart, the X chromosome, is disproportionate in its predisposition for wreaking havoc upon all "the fish of the sea . . . the fowl of the air, and . . . every living thing that moveth upon the earth."

What to do? Indeed, how much more havoc and mayhem can our

stricken planet and its besieged species bear before all the chickens, having escaped from their factory cages, come home to roost?

Might the answer lie with the Wyandot?

Why not?

23

Wanted!
for Crimes against Humanity

THE FOLLOWING BODY COUNTS SERVE TO QUANTIFY THE COMPLICITY of the God of the Old Testament in various campaigns of mass murder. References are included for those who might wish to conduct their own count.

1 Chronicles 11:20	300	Judges 1:4	1,000
1 Chronicles 18:5	22,000	Judges 1:6	70
1 Chronicles 18:12	18,000	Judges 3:29	1,000
1 Chronicles 19:18	47,000	Judges 9:5	70
1 Kings 20:29	100,000	Judges 12:6	42,000
1 Samuel 4:2	4,000	Judges 14:19	30
1 Samuel 4:10	30,000	Judges 15:15	1,000
1 Samuel 18:27	400	1 Maccabees 5:35	8,000
1 Samuel 22:18	85	1 Maccabees 7:16	60
2 Chronicles 13:17	500,000	1 Maccabees 11:48	100,000
2 Chronicles 28:6	120,000	2 Maccabees 5:14	80,000
2 Kings 10:7	70	2 Maccabees 8:24	9,000
2 Kings 14:7	10,000	2 Maccabees 8:30	20,000
2 Samuel 8:5	22,000	2 Maccabees 10:17	20,000
2 Samuel 10:18	54,000	2 Maccabees 10:23	20,000
2 Samuel 21:9	7	2 Maccabees 11:11	12,600
2 Samuel 23:8	800	2 Maccabees 12:4	200
2 Samuel 23:18	300	2 Maccabees 12:19	10,000
Esther 9:6	500	2 Maccabees 12:23	30,000
Esther 9:10	10	2 Maccabees 12:26	25,000
Esther 9:14	10	2 Maccabees 12:28	25,000
Esther 9:15	300	2 Maccabees 13:15	4,000
Esther 9:16	75,000	2 Maccabees 15:27	35,000
Jubilees 38:8	400	Numbers 31:7	250,000

TOTAL: 1,699,212

Not included in this count are those untold millions of men, women, and children who were summarily dispatched (to heaven?) by way of the Great Noahan Flood.

Alas, what god is not tribal; what tribe, not trouble?

24
Guess Who?

LTHOUGH OUR MYSTERY MAN WAS HEAVILY INVOLVED IN THE founding of our nation, he never sought elected office. He was elected to various offices anyway, but on each of those occasions he was essentially conscripted into office by people who knew what an authentic leader was and what a faux leader was not.

Our friend was content to work behind the scenes, and rarely took credit for his ideas or initiatives. At salons and soirées, he was mostly silent, content to listen to what others had to say. He never allowed himself to be drawn into a public argument, and never spoke ill of anyone in public.

On several occasions, our friend drew from his personal fortune, or put it at risk, toward protecting or furthering the public interest. For example, in 1755, when General Braddock arrived in the colonies with a large army to push the French out of the Ohio Valley, the General expected the colonists to supply him with provisions, including horses and wagons. When the colonists balked, and General Braddock threatened seizure, our friend convinced the farmers of Pennsylvania to supply the General with everything he demanded by putting his personal fortune up as collateral.

When Braddock was routed by Indians allied with the French, losing to ambush after ambush two-thirds his officers and one-half his men, his own life in the bargain, our friend was faced with financial ruin. (Fortunately, the royal governor of Pennsylvania ultimately covered our friend's £20,000 surety bond in full.)

Our friend refused to exploit his inventions for financial enrichment. For example, in 1741, he invented the Pennsylvania fireplace and refused to patent it. As a result, the Pennsylvania fireplace—far more efficient and effective than any heating system that preceded it—proliferated throughout the land, to the comfort of many. The inventor collected not a penny.

Our mystery man was the very paragon of open-mindedness, a trait he tirelessly attempted to cultivate in others, through his lending libraries, his newspaper, his Almanacks, his Junto, his College of Pennsylvania (now the University of Pennsylvania), his prolific correspondence, and his private persuasion.

Guess who?

25
Liar! Liar!

A THREE-MINUTE EXERCISE:

PART 1.

Over the next sixty seconds, write down all the advertisers you are aware of that assiduously and consistently tell the truth in their ads. That is, they never attempt to manipulate or mislead the viewer in any way. They simply put forth the facts and let the facts speak for themselves.

Ready?

Go!

PART 2.

OK, over the next 60 seconds, write down all the politicians you are aware of who sixty tell the truth no matter what the consequences might be to themselves or their personal interests. They simply put forth the facts and let the facts speak for themselves.

Ready?

Go!

PART 3.

Finally, over the next sixty seconds, write down all the people you are aware of (including yourself, of course) whose résumé you would trust to be absolutely factual. These people would never embellish, hide, or mislead, much less deliberately lie.

They would simply put forth the facts and let the facts speak for themselves.

Ready?

Go!

Is a house of lies any different than a house of cards?

26
Happiness Is . . .

APPINESS IN OUR CULTURE IS LARGELY FOOL'S GOLD PEDDLED BY all manner of hucksters and pied pipers, ranging from auto dealers to fast-food purveyors to televangelists. Drive this car, consume this confection, embrace this religion, make this amount of money, take this vacation, lean into this boardroom, wear these clothes, own this gismo, pursue this career, and you will be happy!

In truth, happiness is not what we experience when we allow our corporal (reptilian) self its ephemeral pleasures, but what we experience when we allow our higher (spiritual) self an enduring fulfillment.

In the West, we have largely conflated pleasure (satiation of desire and appetite) with happiness (attainment of meaning and inner peace). At bottom, however, these oft-confused rewards or payoffs to our pursuit of happiness could not be more different.

Pleasure is inherently fleeting in nature, is often intense (orgasmic), and results from directing the arrow of one's concern inward, toward the self. Happiness, on the other hand, true happiness, is cumulative and enduring in nature, is always modest and quiescent (like moon glow), and results from directing the arrow of one's concern outward, toward others.

Pleasure is good, of course, because it is essential, but pleasure is not fulfillment, is not inner peace, and can never be, in and of itself, quite purpose enough for any particular one of us.

27
Road Kill

THE CONCEPT AND IMAGES OF "ROAD KILL" ARE READY FODDER FOR all manner of jokes, in all manner of venues, except, of course, when the mangled or flattened creature happens to be our Fido or our Puss. In truth, though, isn't the creature mangled or flattened on the roadway *always our* Fido or *our* Puss, even when it's somebody else's, or just a hapless squirrel or skunk?

Indeed, if it is not—that is, if we allow ourselves to become so desensitized to the carnage of critters on our roadways that our only response is to make jokes—what is likely to become the fate of the natural world at large over the next hundred years or so?

As kindreds of every other living thing on Earth (we *all* came from the same Eve cell); as stewards by default of all "the fish of the sea . . . the fowl of the air, and . . . every living thing that moveth upon the earth;" as an integral part of the natural world ourselves; have we no reason or responsibility to be concerned about this issue?

Flash forward. It's Judgment Day. It's the Judgment Day. You are led by two androgynous archangels into a celestial courtroom and are surprised to find sitting behind the judges' bench a skunk, a squirrel, and a 'possum. Each critter is wearing a black robe showing a stark-white tire track imprinted on the front.

Good luck to ya!

28
To What End, Inspiration?

N FRANK CAPRA'S *It's a Wonderful Life*, GEORGE BAILEY (JAMES Stewart) had to make a fundamental choice between the glitter of life in the big city and the glow of life in a small town—between, in other words, a life of materiality and a life of meaning. He chose meaning, by sacrificing his own dreams so others might realize theirs, but he did not realize this at the time. Instead, he increasingly regarded his life a failure, ultimately to the point of despondency. Of course, had George realized the full nature of his choice at the time he made it, there would have been no dramatic tension around which to weave a tale that countless viewers over the years have found inspirational.

To what end, though, all that inspiration, over all those years?

Not just thousands upon thousands of people, but millions upon millions have viewed Frank Capra's Christmas classic since its debut in 1946, in many cases several times over. Likewise, millions upon millions (many of them the same people) have viewed or read Dickens' version of the inspirational Christmas tale, *A Christmas Carol*, also, in many cases, several times over.

Has the world been changed at all? Has the inspiration derived from these deeply moving tales swayed millions upon millions of people to lead lives of meaning versus lives of materiality? Or have all those millions and millions of people simply been as if warmed to a soft glow in a darkened theater only to be returned then into the harsh glare of reality?

29
Time to Say Good-Bye?

WHAT RIGHT DID MR. LINCOLN AND THE NORTH HAVE TO PREVENT the South from breaking away from the Union in 1861? Was it the same right George III had to prevent the American colonies from breaking away from the Empire in 1776?

Did not, in fact, essentially the same end justify essentially the same means in both instances? And might not the Northern States, as well as the Southern States, be better off today had they peaceably gone their separate ways back in 1861—or even earlier—in fact, at the time of the framing of the Constitution, when the infamous Two-Thirds Compromise was rationalized as the glue that would hold the colonies together for all time?

Consider in this regard the deep divides that exist today between roughly the same demographics of 150 years ago over such issues as global climate change, abortion, school prayer, immigration, universal health care, creationism, "big government," "the border wall," social safety nets, environmental degradation, unrestrained drilling, minimum wage, regulation, gay marriage, euthanasia, trickle-down economics, fracting, gun control, and American Exceptionalism, to name only some of the more obvious issues.

Might these deep divides in fact represent irreconcilable differences?

Might it be time to say good-bye—the Blue States to Red States, the Red States to Blue States? Or must we all stay together for the sake of the children?

30
A Bill of Responsibilities

A BILL OF RIGHTS (I, ME, MINE) IMPLIES A BILL OF RESPONSIBILITIES (they, them, theirs). Had the Founding Fathers been Founding Mothers, they might have come up with a Bill of Responsibilities similar to the following:

1. I will take only what I need.
2. I will put back what I do not use.
3. I will get to know my neighbor.
4. I will protect and nurture all children.
5. I will be a steward of the earth.
6. I will attend to my health.
7. I will apologize.
8. I will ask permission.
9. I will offer forgiveness.
10. I will hold myself accountable.
11. I will stay informed.
12. I will think.

Is it too late to add a Bill of Responsibilities to the national scripture? If indeed it is not, who will lead the charge?

Might it be you, you think?

31
The Great Phallus(y)

HUMAN MALES NEED TO FEEL POWERFUL. THERE IS NOTHING intrinsically wrong with this, of course; all human needs and instincts, as in the case of all human thoughts, are benign in and of themselves. The way human males choose to feel powerful, however, is another matter. Take, for example, bearing firearms as a way of feeling powerful. In the case of males playing war with toy guns, there is little possibility of any real harm. In fact, a fair measure of good is likely to result. In the case of males bearing *real* guns, however, there is, without exception, a significant possibility of harm.

The gun lobby tells us that "guns don't kill people, people do." They are, of course, dead wrong. In truth, it is both. It's the gun and it's the person bearing it. The equation is as simple as it is incontrovertible:

$$Gun + Bearer = Bang!$$

No Bearer, no Bang. No gun, no Bang.

Given the nature and density of the modern world, a reasonable person might well ask whether the Second Amendment (enshrining the right to bear arms), as in the case of the Eighteenth Amendment (establishing prohibition), has become an anachronism. In the world of 1789, the average human male needed to bear arms not only for basic survival purposes, but also to be ready for a summons from the captain of the local militia.

That world, however, no longer exists. In truth, in the world in which we now live, guns do not make men powerful; they simply make them more dangerous.

32
Don't Breathe the Air!

SEVERAL YEARS AGO, JOHN BRADSHAW, A DEPENDENCY / RECOVERY evangelist (some would say zealot), was much maligned for claiming that something on the order of ninety-seven percent of all American families were dysfunctional. On the surface of it, this claim would appear to be extravagant indeed, if not downright preposterous.

Then again, picture yourself shut up in a hermetically sealed room (our culture) with, say, a hundred other people. By necessity, you are all breathing the same air (the prevailing beliefs and values), which is being supplied by external sources (Hollywood, Madison Avenue, the media, celebrities, etc.). If the mix of this air should be dominated by materialism and meism (calls to pleasure and self-gratification), while containing only trace amounts of manna and meaning (calls to contribution and fulfillment), what is likely to be the condition of at least ninety-seven of you?

If you have not yet seen Mike Leigh's film *Another Year*, now might be a good time.

33
Fat Attack

W E LIVE IN A TIME WHEN OPPORTUNITIES TO MAKE MEANING are limited and diminishing. In the past, our forebears, especially the more distant of these, had readily available to them two reliable sources of meaning—work and relationship. In our time, however, these ancient wellsprings of meaning have become all but lost to us. Indeed, what do "TGIF," "burnout," "pays the bills," "work to rule," and "early retirement" suggest about the nature of work today. What do "significant other," "ex" "live in," Facebook friend," and "hookup," suggest about the nature of relationship?

In attempting to compensate for the loss of meaning in our lives, many of us have unwittingly fallen into a trap: Confusing psychic emptiness with physical hunger, pleasure with happiness, we have set into motion a vicious cycle, a downward spiral, from which we are finding it increasingly difficult to extricate ourselves: Using the income we derive from work that fails to fulfill us, we attempt to compensate by pleasuring ourselves, largely through the acquisition and consumption of material things, including, if not especially, food. In doing this, however, instead of filling the void within, we inadvertently deepen it. Around and around we go; down-down we go.

One could argue that America's biggest problem today is not terrorism, or a crumbling infrastructure, or the opioid crisis, or even a lack of leadership; rather, it is a woeful lack of meaning in the average person's every-day, moment-to-moment life.

34
On Bullying

POPULAR WISDOM SEEMS TO HAVE IT THAT THE SOLUTION TO OUR growing bullying problem (not to mention a dozen or so other social ills) rests with our schools; in particular, with establishing and enforcing zero-tolerance policies on school grounds. Typically, under such policies, if someone chooses to bully, and their actions are caught on surveillance video, from fifteen different angles, they're "outa here."

But does removing a bully from one venue only to pace him in another solve the problem, or does it simply make a problem for A a problem for B, and eventually for C? In fact, isn't zero tolerance just another form of passing the buck?

To solve our bullying problem, it would seem that we must first—before saddling our schools with the responsibility of solving yet one more intractable social ill—understand why bullies bully. Toward this end, if we were to delve into the lives of typical school-yard bullies, what might we find? Children who are nurtured and cherished? Children who are gently guided and mentored? Children who are made to feel useful and self-confident? Parents who are models of empathy, tolerance, and forbearance? Children who are expected to do their homework every night before doing anything else? Fathers who are actively engaged in the lives of their children?

In fact, isn't bullying simply a symptom of a much deeper ill, one that cannot be solved with facile or politically expedient remedies? If indeed it is, should we as a society continue to look to our schools for a solution to our bullying problem, or should we perhaps start to assess the overall health and well-being of the American family?

Finally, where is it written that a child witnessing another child being bullied must stand by and allow the abuse to go on? Is not a bully only as bold and as powerful as those around him allow him to be? Does it not take but one bystander of courage and moral fiber to organize a militia?

35
The Four Realms (x 2)

A LITTLE ARMCHAIR DEDUCTION, LEAVENED WITH A LITTLE speculation, would suggest a model of reality consisting of four distinct but inseparable realms—the Logical, the Mathematical, the Physical, and (for lack of a better term) the Mystical.

Under this model, the first realm, the Logical, is one-dimensional and consists of the Mother Grammar of all possibility. This realm takes up no space but makes space (and all the rest of reality) not only infinitely possible but infinitely necessary.

The second realm, the Mathematical, is two-dimensional and consists of all mathematical possibility. This realm might be visualized as the surface of a whiteboard on which are written all possible mathematical formulations.

The third realm, the Physical, is three-dimensional and consists of all possible physical reality. This realm might be visualized as an ocean of soap bubbles, of infinite reach, with each bubble representing a unique construct of the Mother Grammar (that is, a unique universe).

The fourth realm, the Mystical, consists of a state of perfect union, or oneness. There is no separation here; only infinite entanglement. One might visualize this realm as a beam of light that, if passed through a prism of a certain kind, would reveal an infinite spectrum of colorations.

The relation among these four realms of reality would appear to be successive, with the one-dimensional realm being the "shadow" of the two-dimensional realm; the two-dimensional realm being the "shadow" of the three-dimensional realm; the three-dimensional realm being the "shadow" of the four-dimensional realm.

Consonant with these four realms, there would appear to be four realms of meaning—the Data Realm, the Information Realm, the Knowledge Realm, and the Wisdom Realm. The relation among these latter realms would also appear to be successive, with information deriving of data, knowledge of information, wisdom of knowledge.

Alas, might we have here two faces on the same Eve?

36
Dumb, Dumber, Dumbest

DUMB

- Keeping a balance on a credit card.
- Not getting enough sleep.
- Texting through science class.
- Eating beyond necessity.
- Using television as a babysitter.
- Taking the elevator instead of the stairs.
- Waiting for God to whisper in your ear.

DUMBER

- Texting while driving.
- Not reading a daily newspaper.
- Voting for any candidate who ends his stump speech with "God bless America."
- Giving your children a cellphone instead of two cans and a string.
- Driving any automobile that gets less than 40 mpg.
- Taking photos instead of immersing yourself in the moment.
- Waiting for your ship to come in.

DUMBEST

- Expecting a merit raise.
- Not saving enough for retirement.
- Allowing politicians to set their own salary and benefits.
- Not reading at least one book a day to your children.
- Being wired a.k.a. connected 24 x 7.
- Not pursuing at least one labor of love.
- Buying diet books.

37
Why I'm Not Voting
This Year

HAVE LONG ADMIRED THE CHILD IN HANS CHRISTIAN ANDERSEN'S *The Emperor's New Clothes* who dared point out to the throng that the Emperor was strutting around without any clothes on. Everyone else in the crowd that day was effectively part of a conspiracy of silence— see naught, say naught. (One can get insights from this kind of thing into how something like the Holocaust could happen . . . over and over again.)

In the face of an unspoken expectation of conformity, Andersen's nameless child performed two heroic acts: He (or she) allowed himself to <u>see</u> the truth when apparently nobody else was willing to; and he (or she) allowed himself to <u>speak</u> the truth when apparently no one else was willing to (including, presumably, the child's parents).

Which, strange as it might seem, brings me to the reason I'm not voting this year. Simply put, I'm not voting this year because no one running for office is worthy of my vote—

No one who is willing to point out that the real problem behind the failure of our schools today is not a lack of resources or programs or reforms, but an all-pervasive, culturally-driven anti-intellectualism that forces children at an early age to choose between being included and being learned;

No one who is willing to point out that our system of governance is fatally flawed in that it makes it almost impossible for average citizens, like you and me, to hold public office;

No one who is willing to point out that every individual right, written or unwritten, guaranteed or not guaranteed, comes with a commensurate responsibility;

No one who is willing to point out that our first Black President ended any prospect of being regarded a moral leader on a par with Martin Luther King or Nelson Mandela the moment he accepted the Nobel Peace Prize for no greater deed than being not Bush?

Now that I think about it, there's another reason I'm not voting this year. In growing up in a double-alcoholic home, I attained a certain body of wisdom that tells me that continuing to vote for people who are addicted to power is not the way to help one's self, one's country, or one's world.

38
Garbage In, Garbage Out

WHY IS IT THAT SEEMINGLY EVERY EDUCATOR, POLITICIAN, and public-policy "expert" in the country does not seem to understand that if you put reluctant, distracted, undisciplined, ill-prepared, unruly, unkempt, incurious, anti-intellectual students in a classroom, *any* classroom, you're not going to get "trustworthy, loyal, helpful, friendly, courteous, kind, obedient, cheerful, thrifty, brave, clean, and reverent" citizens on the other end? As the old saying goes: garbage in, garbage out.

The problem, of course, is that while every one of those educators, politicians, and public-policy experts mentioned above sees the "garbage-out" part of the problem—to wit, ever increasing numbers of high-school graduates who can't read, multiply, write, or think—they do not see, or they refuse to admit they see, the "garbage-in" part. And because they do not see this part of the problem, they keep coming up with such hare-brained solutions to the problem as:

The Open Classroom

The New Match

The Self-Esteem /
Up with Everybody
Movement

Zero Tolerance

Algebra for Everybody

No Child Left Behind

Computer-Aided
Education (CAE)

Race to the Top

Massive Open Online
Courses (MOOCs)

Common Core

Underlying most of these silver-bullet remedies is the unspoken assumption that the cause of most of our educational ills today lies *not* with failing students—or failing parents, or a failing sports-crazed, anti-intellectual society—but with failing schools.

Reluctant, distracted, undisciplined, ill-prepared, unruly, unkempt, incurious, anti-intellectual students don't fail; the best-funded schools on the planet do!

Don't you love it?

39

What's the Rush?

WHERE IS IT WRITTEN THAT ALL TESTS MUST BE TIMED? The reigning presumption, of course, is that tests need to be timed in order to prepare future workers for a dog-eat-dog world in which the race always goes to the swift. There is at least a modicum of truth in this presumption, but not nearly enough to support the notion that everyone benefits from tests being universally taken under duress. Haste still makes waste, and let's not forget what happened between the tortoise and the hare.

The truth of the matter is that tests are timed largely (if not wholly) for the convenience of the test-*givers*, who are loath to be held hostage to a bunch of plodding numb-skulls. For them, the less time test-takers are allowed to sweat puddles, the more time they themselves will have to do other things. Over the years, as in the case of the seventh-inning stretch, the practice of timing tests has taken on a life of its own.

Many of us out here in the dog-eat-dog world are inherently slow. Everything about us is slow. We eat slowly, we think slowly. We metabolize slowly. We walk slowly. We remember slowly. We live in the slow lane (except when driving, of course). For us, being fast—being *compelled* to be fast—is torture. It is also a sure way of missing the full measure of who we really are, and what we're really capable of.

Force us to go fast and bad things happen. For example, one day when I was in first grade, I could not understand what my teacher, Winnie Sullivan Blum, god bless her, was asking us to do. She was going too fast for my plodding little tortoise of a brain to keep up. I became so agitated I wet my pants. I made a very large, very noticeable puddle on the floor, adding volume and tincture to the puddle of sweat already accumulated there. I had to walk home in my wet clothes. Apparently someone driving me home would have been too fast.

40
On (and Off) Poetry

HAVE OFTEN WONDERED WHAT THE EFFECT MIGHT BE IF MODERN poets tended to strive for lucidity rather than for . . . well, let's call it "profundity," to be kind. When I was young, hopelessly inchoate, and easily intimidated, I found the experience of reading poetry not only maddeningly frustrating, but painfully diminishing. I could not even begin to understand most of what I was reading (over and over again) and felt, of course, that it had to be *my* fault. How could it be otherwise? I wouldn't be asked to read what was torturing me if it were not comprehensible to everyone on the planet except me.

The problem was, of course, I simply wasn't up to the task. I was a dummy.

As I grew older, however, and the analytical part of my brain gradually grew into its own, and I gathered courage enough in the face of those things that heretofore had intimidated or diminished me, I became more critical of both what I read and who wrote it. My tolerance for "profundity," in other words, not to mention for "profunditors," greatly diminished.

To be fair, poetry is what it is largely because of the constraints it must accommodate either in part or in full. Taken together, these constraints (rhythm, rhyme, meter, pattern, form) unavoidably lead to convoluted constructions, fractured grammar, tortured semantics, jarring non sequiturs, and a complete or near-complete lack of punctuation.

Even so, one gets the feeling in reading the occasional poem in *Atlantic* or the *New Yorker* that a great deal of the opacity one encounters in poetry is deliberate, a ploy toward gaining a reputation for being able to suck ambrosia from a stone without benefit of a straw. Clarity in these cases is not only not a goal, one suspects; it is, in fact, to be avoided at all costs. To be clear, alas, might well reveal that one does not, in actuality, have all that much to say.

(Come to think of it, there are a few politicians in this country who quite possibly might have the same problem.)

41
Algebra for Everybody

NOT LONG AGO, AMERICA'S EDUCATION ESTABLISHMENT, IN YET another stunning exhibition of pedagogical genius, came up with a program, Algebra for All, that would require every ninth grader (or earlier) to be exposed to the power and majesty of algebra. The assumption underlying this innovation was twofold: (1) that every student in America was capable of succeeding in such a program, and (2) that every student would substantially benefit from such a program.

In effect, Algebra for All (Everybody) would place every ninth-grader in America, no matter what his or her circumstances and/or natural aptitudes might be, on a track to college and thereby limitless opportunity.

I think I can. I think I can . . .

One suspects that the innovators behind Algebra for Everybody were the same wunderkind who gave us No Child Left Behind (Success for Everyone) and the Race to the Top (Victory for Everyone). One suspects further that it was the forebears of these same wunderkind who gave us Self-Esteem for Everybody and the Open Classroom for Everybody; and that it was *their* forebears who gave us Memorization for Everybody Penmanship for Everyone and Shakespeare for Everybody.

Underlying these Up with Everybody programs, one senses, is a deep reverence for, and belief in, massive democratization projects as the best (and only?) means of ensuring equal opportunity for all. But is algebra *truly* for everyone? Is Shakespeare *truly* for everyone? Might these programs have in fact done, or be doing, more harm than good? Is there not in fact a common naiveté (a.k.a. blissful thinking) shared among them?

In the case of Algebra for Everybody, if all comers, all stripes, all abilities, were placed in the same classroom, where maybe fifteen percent of the students actually wanted to be there, what likely would be the result? How many of the coerced students would, realistically, succeed? What likely would be the consequence to those who failed?

What likely would be the effect on teachers having to simultaneously address widely varying capability and motivation levels? Where would all the qualified teachers come from? How many students would any one teacher be required to serve at any one time?

In other words, what likely would be and not be?

42

To Viktor
Go the Spoils

W HEN VIKTOR YANUKOVYCH, THEN PRESIDENT OF UKRAINE, fled the country for his life, he left behind a palace reminiscent of Versailles in its manifest excess. The existence of this palace, complete with its own zoo, came as a revelation to the Ukrainian people, who had been kept in the dark about both it and the corruption that had spawned it, but it could not have come as a surprise to them. After all, European history is rife with autocrats of one sort or another being ensconced in palaces of various sorts and sizes—great houses, mansions, dachas, villas, chateaus, citadels, redoubts, castles, and the like. Where there was an autocrat—or, perhaps more accurately, where there was a larger-than-life ego—one could expect to find it ensconced in a larger-than-life domicile—or, perhaps more accurately, a proportionate monument.

Although we in the New World do not have quite the history with autocrats as the Old World has, we have had, and still have, no shortage of egoists ensconced in a palace of one sort or another. Our president resides in a Palladian palace, for example; our Congress in a Neoclassical temple; and we have many a Wall Street tycoon or business mogul "simultaneously" ensconced in a penthouse in New York, a chalet in Vail, a beach house in Costa Rica, and a villa in Tuscany. And then, of course, closer to home (so to say), we have many a parvenu ensconced in a Starter Castle or a McMansion.

Beyond the Old and New Worlds, the beat goes on. There's the Taj Mahal, the Forbidden City, Machu Picchu, the Pyramids, and sundry other extravagances—on and on—through, in fact, all of human history. One suspects, in fact, that 400,000 years ago, the biggest ego in each tribe dwelled in the biggest tree or the biggest cave or the biggest whatever.

In fact, isn't bigness the primary metric by which human beings measure power and authority? Why does the pope sit in a castle on a hill in unabashed defiance of the example set by the humble prophet he is supposed to be emulating? Would anyone pay attention to him if he did not? Would anybody listen to the American President if he lived in a tent on the Mall? Would anyone listen to a politician who arrived at a campaign rally in a Honda Fit instead of a limo half a block long?

43
Double Standard

O<small>N THE SURFACE OF THINGS, IT WOULD CERTAINLY SEEM THAT</small> paying men more than women who possess essentially the same abilities and experience is a gross violation of fairness. If something looks like a duck, walks like a duck, quacks like a duck, it's a duck; right? We know gross unfairness when we see it. Right?

Yes and no. Here's the problem:

We are assuming above that, in addition to being equal in experience and ability, the men and women holding down the same job are equal in all other respects relevant to the workplace. But are they? Let's say you are male and own a company named Web Wonks that designs high-end Websites. In your Design Department, you employ twenty people, ten men and ten women, all of whom are equal in experience and ability. You are paying the men an average of $50 per hour; the women an average of $45 per hour. In other words, you're a sexist pig and, effectually, a shameless thief.

Actually, you are the person who is ultimately responsible for the survival of your business. You are not part of the social safety net. What you are, alas, is a warrior in a dog-eat-dog world whose concerns are but two, revenue and cost, and whose overarching mission is to maximize the former and minimize the latter.

In minimizing the latter, you need to take into consideration all relevant costs, not just the most-obvious ones. Less-obvious costs might include some that are, unavoidably, gender-specific. For example, women (single mothers in particular) typically require more time off than men do to deal with child-care needs, or the care of elderly family member. This is a cost. They also experience more debilitating headaches than men do. This is a cost. And so on.

The bottom line here is that any owner or manager of a business who does not factor all costs, including gender-specific costs, into the overall profitability of his or her firm, is going to find himself or herself one day in deep doo-doo. This is not to say that women are not discriminated against in the male-dominated world of business; we all know the deal. It is only to say that there can be a not-always-recognized logic behind what appears to be a patently unfair double standard.

44
Alien-Nation

A WOMAN WHO HAD BEEN LIVING IN A QUIET PONTIAC-MICHIGAN neighborhood was recently found dead in her garage. Her body had mummified. She had been dead for six years! In other words, for six years this woman had not been seen or even glimpsed of and no one had taken notice. For six years this woman's mail had been piling up at the post office and no one had taken notice. For six years this woman had not filed a tax return and no one had taken notice. For six years this woman's yard had been left fallow and no one had taken notice. For six years this woman had not turned on a light and no one had taken notice. Only when Pia Farrenkopf's bank account finally ran dry, and certain parties no longer received their automatic payments, did anyone take notice.

An extreme example, for sure, but does it not serve to make a fair point? Are we not becoming a nation of strangers? Are we not becoming ever more separated and alienated from each other? Are we not looking after each other less and less? Are we not increasingly going it alone? And is not technology a big part of the problem?

Take, for example, the Internet—texting, friending, liking, tweeting, instagramming, surfing, snapchatting. Do these technology-enabled activities tend to foster rich, meaningful relationships, or do they do the opposite? Take the ATM and online banking. Because of these two conveniences, we don't know anybody at our bank. We can't call Shirley three minutes before closing on a Friday afternoon and ask her to cover an inadvertent overdraw for us. Because of Amazon.com, we don't know anybody at the mom-and-pop bookstore on Sycamore, and they don't know us, or what we like to read, and so we can't talk books and ideas or about each other's latest bout with shingles. Because of there being a TV in every bedroom, we don't watch the same programs as families, or build the same pop-cultural references, so we have that much less in common to share and discuss and build memories on. Because of GPS, we no longer get lost and experience chance meetings or serendipitous discoveries.

And then there is individualized music and games in the SUV, instead of group discovery and conversation. And then there is computer-based instruction instead of classroom interaction. And then there are self-service checkouts. And then . . .

45

Master Race

THE TEACHER IN ONE OF MY GRADUATE-SCHOOL ENGLISH CLASSES, a Maine Yankee self-exiled to the Midwest, once declared, with a twinkle in his eye, that there was no irony in Iowa. In hindsight, I think Professor Huntress made this statement largely because he liked the alliterative aspect of it. Even so, I had lived in Iowa long enough at that point to appreciate that he probably had a point. Many Iowans are of German descent and Germans are not, according to lore anyway, known for their appreciation of, much less participation in, things ironic.

One German in particular stands out in this regard.

Back in the early twentieth century, Adolf Hitler somehow got it into his head that Germans (and select other Europeans) were Aryans by race, and that Aryans were inherently superior to all other races on Earth. Unfortunately, Herr Hitler also got it into his head that the purity of the Aryan race was under threat from certain unsavory (dark complexioned) elements, namely Jews and Gypsies. He thereafter took it upon himself, as Aryan Über Alles (not to mention Führer Über Alles) to save the Aryans (a.k.a. the Master Race) from an insidious corruption.

Given what appeared to be an incurious nature, it is unlikely that Hitler had, at this time, ever heard of natural or artificial selection. If he had, he very likely would have decided against participating in what was to become one of history's greatest ironies.

When Hitler began his campaign to cleanse Germany (and subsequently the rest of Europe) of unsavory elements, many Jews were able, by exercise of their wits, to escape not only to live another day but to procreate another day, just as many of their forebears had been able to do in the face of past pogroms. Many if not most of those Jews who survived Hitler's genocide immigrated to the U.S., where today they make up only about five percent of the general population but are hugely over-represented in almost every profession one can name, including literature, the arts, academe, journalism, the sciences, law, medicine, business, research, and finance.

As for the Aryans, there hasn't been a sighting in several years now, but rumor has it they are holed up somewhere in Iowa waiting for the Second Coming of the Der Führer.

46
Half-Time
at the Super Bowl

A HOST OF NEAR-NAKED ABORIGINES, THEIR FACES SMEARED WITH ash and blood, are dancing and whooping against the backdrop of a crackling fire. The night sky is moonless; the ambient darkness featureless. The very ground seems to resonate to a heavy beating of drums. Several attendants begin to prod and stir the fire such as to create lofting bursts of sparks and embers.

The gathering roars.

Fast forward 100,000 years.

The stadium has been darkened to eerie effect. A host of near-naked aborigines, their faces smeared as if with ash and blood, are stomping and screaming against a backdrop of flashing lights. The very air seems to resonate to a heavy beating of drums. Suddenly the sky erupts with explosions of sound and light.

The crowd roars.

47

Too Big
to Give a Damn

N 2009, THE U.S. SUFFERED ONE OF ITS WORST FINANCIAL CRISES IN its history.

Thousands of people were complicit in selling subprime mortgages to people who could not afford them but were assured they could. Thousands of people were complicit in falsifying the documentation and assurances used to support the affordability of these subprime mortgages. Thousands of people were complicit in packaging these subprime mortgages into complex securities that were fraudulently valued, fraudulently rated, and fraudulently represented.

As a result, millions of people lost their homes. Millions of people lost their jobs. Millions of people lost all hope of ever retiring. Millions of people lost their health (and in some cases, their life) to stress and despondency. Millions of people lost all faith in their government and their "leaders."

No one went to jail.

No one said they were sorry.

No one offered recompense

Nothing changed.

Pretty much the same thing had gone on in France up until July 14, 1789, on which day heads began to roll—down the street.

Things changed.

48
Not One of Us

HUMAN BEINGS ARE PROBABLY AS TRIBAL IN INSTINCT AS ANY species could ever be. At any particular moment, any particular one of us can identify ourselves as being a member of not one, not a dozen, but likely several dozen tribes of one sort or another. For example, we might identify as being an American citizen, a member of Red Sox Nation, a member of the Republican Party, an Episcopalian, a UVM grad, a member of a particular condo association, a member of a particular book club, an employee of a particular company, a member of a particular department within a particular company, a patron of a particular bookstore, a patron of a particular pub, and so on and so on. In each instance, our tribal affiliation divides our world into two groups: Us and Them.

Of course, for any particular person, the intensity of his affiliations will vary widely, depending on a host of factors, including degree of identification, history of affiliation, and benefits (emotional and physical) gained.

By inclination, we tend to make our affiliations known to others, strangers in particular, using some kind of tacit communication. For example, we might wear a Red Sox cap to advertise our affiliation with Red Sox Nation. Likewise, we might wear a certain kind of ring to signal affiliation with a secret society. Evolutionary logic would suggest we engage in this kind of behavior for two reasons: (1) to invite fellow members of our tribe to step forward and establish solidarity with us; and (2) to warn nonmembers they might well be regarded as a threat.

How powerful can our tribal impulses be? A few years ago, Bryan Stow, a paramedic and father of two, was nearly beaten to death outside Dodger Stadium by two Dodger fans. As a result of severe injuries to his brain, Stow lost motor skills in his arms and hands, lost his ability to walk, lost his ability to carry on a normal conversation, lost his ability to control his bodily functions, and lost his ability to care for himself.

His offence?

He had been rooting for the San Francisco Giants.

49
Greed Is Good

NIKITA KHRUSHCHEV'S SHOE-BANGING BRAGGADOCIO TO THE contrary, capitalism has pretty much vanquished communism and established itself as the world's most successful economic ideology. When you think about it, though, how could it have turned out otherwise? In the cause of creating material wealth, which, to the human psyche, represents survival itself, capitalism harnesses the enormous energy of self-interest, while communism (as well as socialism, its kissing cousin) does the very opposite.

It would seem then that, given its ever-growing success, capitalism must eventually carry everyone on the planet to economic Nirvana. But will it? Or is there a dark side to this moon? Isaac Newton, scientist, might remind us in this regard that for every action there is an equal and opposite reaction, while Isaiah, prophet, might remind us there is a valley for every mountain, and Milton Friedman, economist, might remind us there's no free lunch. In other words, before we allow ourselves to get carried away with the seeming boundless ability of capitalism to deliver prosperity to all, we might want to take a step or two back.

Inherent to capitalism, we can now "see," is a form of myopia that manifests in two ways: (1) in the form of bottom-line thinking, and (2) in the form of the tragedy of the commons. In regard to bottom-line thinking, capitalism focuses on achieving as much gain in the short term as possible—bigger profits, larger market share, etc.—without attaching any meaningful scruples to the means of achievement, as indeed is generally the case whenever any mortal thing sees itself as continually under threat. Actually, capitalism sees itself not so much as continually under threat as continually at war, with everything at stake. Which leads us to the tragedy of the commons.

In its nearsightedness, capitalism takes no notice of, or responsibility for, any of the negative consequences it causes in its drive to maximize its survivability. Hence, rivers get polluted, groundwater gets contaminated, global warming gets triggered, soil gets depleted, species get exterminated. All such consequences remain outside capitalism's circle of concern, at least until such time there is sufficient blow back to singe the seat of capitalism's pants, at which point it might well be too late for there to be any meaningful change in attitude or behavior among all concerned.

50
Pogo Rules

I N THE EYES OF THE IRS AND U.S. LAW, A CORPORATION IS A "PERSON." While this view may be a convenience to the IRS and the courts, not to mention a lawyer or two, the rest of us cannot escape the fact that, in order for a corporation to be a person in anything other than the titular sense, it must have, besides a head, a heart and a soul. How many corporations might we collectively name, however, that manifest, in behavior and attitude, the guiding presence of anything even remotely resembling a heart or a soul?

GM? JPMorgan? Monsanto? Wells Fargo? Sprint? Duke Energy? Pfizer? Facebook? Exxon Mobil? Delta Airlines? Comcast? Amazon? AT&T?

What every corporation is, in the fullest sense (by nature of the beast, so to say), is a hydra-like creature of at least nine heads, with each head representing a specific entity of self-interest, to wit: Managers. Directors. Stockholders. Employees. Suppliers. Marketers. Dealers. Lenders. Customers.

In effect, then, GM, JPMorgan, Monsanto, and the rest (to include every corporate "person" on the planet) can only be as responsible or as moral or as ethical as its various stake-holders individually and collectively require it to be.

In other words, as Pogo once famously said, "We have met the enemy and they is us."

51
Celebrity Status

WHY ARE WE SO FIXATED ON CELEBRITIES? WHY DO WE SEEK them out? Why do we beg for their autographs? Why do we shoot selfies outside their rumored places of residence? Why do we monitor their tweets? Why do we hang on their very public word? Why do we try to make ourselves look like them? Why do we memorialize them with icons and wall-hangings of various sorts?

It may have come about thusly . . .

A long, long time ago, on a savannah far, far away, at least one of our ancient ancestors discovered the power of the suck-up (alliance). Instead of maintaining a wary distance, this ancestor learned to flatter the alpha de jour into including him or her in a sort of symbiotic alliance. In exchange for being assured of social inclusion and physical protection, our enterprising ancestor provided the alpha with worshipful attention, loyal service, and, in the case of female enterprisers, carnal favors.

In more recent times, the possibility of our ingratiating ourselves into a real suck-up with a real alpha for real social inclusion and real physical protection has all but disappeared. Even so, we can pursue a symbolic (or fantasy) alliance with any number of perceived alphas, toward gaining at least the illusion of real social stature and real physical protection. All we need do is simply allow ourselves to become fixated.

Obsessed.

The rest will take care of itself.

52
Friends for Life

W E ARE MASSIVELY CONNECTED IN OUR TIME IN ONE SENSE; massively dis-connected in another. We are massively connected primarily by way of modern communications systems: Internet, iPhone, Facebook, Twitter, Instagram, Snapchat, Skype, et al. Within seconds, we can be in lingual contact with almost any other human being on the planet. We are also massively connected today by way of modern transportation systems: automobile, airplane, metro, Acela, et al. Within hours, we can be standing side by side with almost any other human being on the planet.

We are massively dis-connected in our time by way of a slew of factors, including class, wealth, education, expectation, career, neighborhood, belief, culture, experience, gender, race, ethnicity, et al. Of course, this has always been the case. What is new, and ominous, is degree and scale. Many mere differences of the past have grown into gaping chasms over time and never now the twain shall meet.

Unfortunately, being massively connected in the physical sense (by phone, by Internet) can foster an illusion of being massively connected in the emotional / spiritual sense. Many people today, in fact, essentially equate having a multitude of virtual "friends" with having a multitude of "real" friends, the kind you can count on at a moment's notice to take care of FiFi while you're attending Uncle Jack's third wedding. Their "proof in the pudding" in this regard is the number of Facebook "likes" they can boast of.

53
The Gander-ites
vs.
the Goose-ites

HAVE WE BALKANIZED OURSELVES OUT OF ANY MEANINGFUL notion of nationhood ("from sea to shining sea')? Is what is good for the gander-ites in New York State today likely to be what is good for the goose-ites in Wyoming? Is a young man packing heat in the first-mentioned venue, for instance, of the same concern as a young man toting a shotgun in the second? My sense is that passing universal gun laws to apply equally in all instances would be pure folly. In the short term, it would spawn intense animosity and resistance; in the longer term, open rebellion.

Might we invoke here, in way of example, the Stamp Act of 1765?

The same is true, I suspect, of abortion, school prayer, creationism, global warming, same-sex marriage, and a hundred other such issues. The only realistic way to settle these issues to the satisfaction of all (most) concerned, in each instance, would seem to be through some kind of localization, whereby every state, region, or community (the latter of a certain size and sensibility) would decide for itself what was best for itself. In a highly diverse (fragmented) society, one size cannot fit all.

54
Never Again!

I N THE AFTERMATH OF THE HOLOCAUST, IN WHICH SIX MILLION JEWS were gassed or starved to death, oaths of moral outrage could be heard around the globe.

Never again!

The entire world would rise up as one and crush the monsters into oblivion

We humans appear to be far better at forgetting, however, than at remembering. In just the past forty years alone, for example, we have borne witness to the Killing Fields of Cambodia (1 million dead), the Ugandan genocide (800,000 to 1 million dead), and the Bosnian cleansing (100,000 to 200,000 dead).

Did the Moral West rise up as one in the face of these atrocities and force "Never Again" on those responsible?

Did the Jews, the one people you would expect to lead the charge against such atrocities, send an army?

Did either party do anything more than respond with a few conscience-abetting tokenisms? During the Bosnian cleansing, for example, the Dutch government sent a small contingent of "peacekeepers" to protect ethnic Bosnians in Srebrenica. When the Serbian General in charge of that area, Ratko Mladić, demanded that the Dutch peacekeepers turn 8,000 ethnic Bosnians over to the Serbs, the Dutch, outnumbered and out gunned, complied. General Mladić thereupon ordered every man and boy among those 8,000 souls be put to death.

Never again?

55
On Retirement

Y FATHER BUILT A MARINA IN CAPE VINCENT, NY, BACK in the early sixties. Cape Vincent, a tiny village of 795, sits where the St. Lawrence River meets Lake Ontario, about three hours north and east of Rochester. At the time, Rochester was home to such mega-employers as Kodak, Xerox, and Bausch & Lomb. My father had noticed that many of the blue-collar employees affiliated with these companies owned cabin cruises for which they needed safe harbor, not to mention fuel, storage, and maintenance. My father happily accommodated them with his marina.

Most of these blue-collar workers were the beneficiaries of liberal pension plans that would allow them to retire comfortably, which, over the 1960s and 70s, they did, in droves. Life was good.

But then things changed, as they are prone to do. Both Kodak and Xerox missed the boat, so to say, regarding technology changes in their respective industries, and were unable to compensate. The savings and loan crisis followed, and then the dot-com bubble, and then the Great Recession. Downsizing and outsourcing began to thrive; employment diminished; pensions all but disappeared. Aspirations sunk.

And not just in Rochester. The economy as a whole suffered a massive transformation. As a result, the ways and means to retirement—not just for blue-collar workers, but for most workers—were transformed from each employee showing up at work every day for thirty years, to each one accumulating enough money on his or her own to fund 25 to 30 years of retirement, with little help from the stock market, which, in the days of the guaranteed pension, could be counted on to appreciate an average of ten percent per year.

Unfortunately, the pension-less, forced-to-go-it-alone employee of today has managed to save, on average, a grand total of $24k for retirement. How much is needed? Most financial advisors agree that, for a sixty-five-year-old couple faced with funding a twenty-five to thirty-year retirement, it would take a nest egg of between $1M and $1.5M for them to live in modest comfort, without fear of running out of money during their lifetime.

Alas, we have come a long way from a cabin cruiser in every slip.

56
Why I'm Not Doing Xmas This Year

No, it's not because I'm Jewish or Muslim or Buddhist or Confucian. I'm a French-Irish ex-Catholic. And, no, it's not because of any need to "put Christ back into Christ-mas." (There's no doubt in my mind that if Jesus had any say in the matter, he'd opt out of not only *doing* Christmas, but *being* Christmas, out of sheer embarrassment.)

I'm not doing Christmas this year because, at 75, it finally occurred to me that Christmas fits the definition of insanity to a T—doing the same thing over and over again expecting a different result.

Think about it. Isn't this what most of us have been doing all these years—entering into the Christmas madness every year (a little earlier each time) expecting that, this time it's going to be different? This year, by golly, we're going to be transformed into giddy, giggly fools, just like ol' Ebenezer himself.

Let's face it. Christmas is a disaster. No, it's full-blown horror. It reminds us how unhappy we all really are. It reminds us how superficial our relationships really are. It reminds us how poor we really are. It reminds us how much we hate being manipulated. It reminds us how much we dislike feeling guilty. It reminds us how much we hate confronting those red kettles parked outside every supermarket on the planet.

OK, the good news. I think I've got a way I can be lured back to "the Christmas Spirit" and maybe bring you with me. Here it is: We hold a national Secret Santa Lottery. We put all 312,731,079 of our names, including those of all those undocumented terrorists and rapists the Republicans hate so much, in a very large hat, and then we enlist a cadre of humble Hollywood celebrities to draw names on everyone's behalf. The name drawn on your behalf is the only person you have to gift. What's more, you don't have to buy anything. In fact, you can't. It's against the rules. What you have to do is you have to *make* something. Yep, that's right. You have to make something with your own hands. Your own heart. Your own soul. And then you have to send it to the giftee (by UPS, because the post Office is soon going to be out of business) with no return address. That's it. That's the new (old) Christmas.

Are you in?

57
On Humility

A S THE AUTHOR OF A NOVEL FEATURING BEN FRANKLIN, I AM often asked which political party Ben would affiliate with if he were to come back. The answer of course is "neither." Ben Franklin was a child of the Enlightenment. He was a free thinker. He believed in the primacy of knowledge and reason over dogma and reflex. Hence the public libraries. The Almanacks. The American Philosophical Society. The Pennsylvania Gazette. The bagatelles ("The Speech of Miss Polly Baker" et al). Franklin would never have allowed any corpus of belief, from any quarter, to do his thinking for him.

Franklin also believed in the primacy of compromise (the art of giving a little to get a little) over absolutism. He would never have allied himself with any party or group that claimed to know what was best or right on every issue, and that refused to compromise its position in any regard, to any degree. Just how much Franklin believed in compromise, the necessity of it, is demonstrated in the speech he delivered (via James Wilson) just before the vote was to be taken on ratifying the U.S. Constitution. The outcome of this vote was, at the time, very much in doubt:

> I confess that there are several parts of this constitution which I do not at present approve, but I am not sure I shall never approve them; for having lived long, I have experienced many instances of being obliged by better information, or fuller consideration, to change opinions even on important subjects [that] I once thought right, but found to be otherwise. It is therefore that the older I grow, the more apt I am to doubt my own judgment, and to pay more respect to the judgment of others.
>
> Most men indeed as well as most sects in religion think themselves in possession of all truth, and that wherever others differ from them it is so far error. Steele[,] a Protestant[,] in a dedication[,] tells the Pope that the only difference between our churches in their opinions of the

certainty of their doctrines is the Church of Rome is infallible and the Church of England is never in the wrong.

All but shocking here, I think you will agree, is a palpable sense of humility underlying the whole of Franklin's call for compromise.

Humility?

In a public figure?

Holy Moly, Batman!

58
Student-Athletes
& the Second Amendment

THE U.S. IS THE ONLY INDUSTRIALIZED NATION IN THE WORLD in which its schools, from the secondary level through the university level, sponsor what amounts to professional athletics. This reality reflects a set of values that has long placed physical skills in America above cognitive skills; winning over learning.

The U.S. was not founded by scholars, philosophers, artists, writers, and such, but by farmers, trappers, miners, track layers, canal diggers, and such. The latter were not widely interested in their children acquiring a formal education, especially the kind of education favored by European élites. Instead, they were interested in their children acquiring the kind of skills that would protect them from starvation, and the kind of skills that would keep them from losing their scalp.

If we couple this survival-based mindset with the anti-intellectual attitude that many early settlers brought to the New World with them, the marginalization of intellectuals (eggheads, geeks, Eineys) in America begins to make perfect sense. So, too, do million-dollar, state-of-the-art high-school stadiums; embarrassingly high-paid coaches; sexual, social, and academic double-standards for athletes; sporting extravaganzas held on school nights; and, of course, the largely unacknowledged joke the term "student athlete" has become.

Once upon a time, all school-based sports were both local and universal; that is, they were intramural and they involved every able-bodied student. (My great aunt played basketball back in the early 1900s.) As in the Athens of Aristotle, sports were part of a larger regime designed to perfect the whole of each person. And for a while, a relatively brief while to be sure, this regime worked well. But then, given the context in which universal exercise attempted to fulfill its mission, school-based sports soon took on a life of their own. In short, they were co-opted by a mindset and attitude that, as in the example of the cosmic microwave background radiation, has persisted into every corner of the American universe.

59
The Power of Scale

MANY THINGS THAT ARE WORKABLE IN SMALL NUMBERS—THAT IS, on a small scale—are not workable in large numbers—that is, on a large scale.

Take, for example, the practice of using the world's lakes and streams as sewers and dumping grounds. As long as the number of polluters remains relatively low, and the volume of uncompromised fresh water remains relatively high, there can be little danger of our fouling ourselves into extinction. There would always be local damage, of course—a polluted pond here, a fouled creek there—but no global or lasting damage.

Increase the scale, however, and everything changes. Regarding our example, increase the human population from a few hundred thousand, as was the case when our distant ancestors inhabited parts of Africa, to the 7.4 billion global dwellers of today. How much waste and effluvia can 7.4 billion people dump into the world's lakes and streams before these essential sources of fresh water become permanently poisoned?

QUESTION: Who's in charge? Who's setting local and global policy regarding such issues as pollution and despoliation? The women of the world?

Once upon a time, one person acting alone could do little lasting damage either to the natural world or to his/her local community. His/her capacity for destruction was limited by the scale of the means of destruction available to him. Compare a handmade spear or knife, for example, to an AR-15 assault rifle with high-capacity magazines. Indeed, we have entered an era in which one person, acting alone, can hack into a power grid and bring darkness and terror to millions of people. We have entered an era in which one person, acting alone, can storm a school, a movie theater, or a night club and slaughter scores of innocent people in seconds.

QUESTION: Who's in charge? Who's setting local and global policy regarding such issues as the availability and possession of firearms? The women of the world?

60
Litany of Shame

A S IS BECOMING INCREASINGLY DIFFICULT TO IGNORE, HUMAN males have been in charge of pretty much everything over the past 400 millennia, and have pretty much made a mess of things. Let us count a few of the ways:

Lusting after political and economic power

Wielding such power over the weak and the vulnerable

Favoring expediency over ethics

Pushing innumerable species into extinction

Carrying on mindless 'blood feuds'

Allowing millions of children to perish of starvation and preventable disease

Degrading and despoiling the natural world

Waging endless war

Inventing ever-more-lethal weapons for waging ever-more endless war

Marginalizing and mistreating women

Inventing homophobic and misogynist religions

Condoning 'honor killings'

Normalizing rape

Begetting and abandoning legions of 'fatherless' children

The problem here, given the consistency of this sad legacy, not to mention its enormity, would appear to be inherent to the Y chromosome, which, although puny in physical size relative to its Queen Bee counterpart, the X chromosome, would appear to be predisposed toward wreaking havoc upon all "the fish of the sea . . . the fowl of the air, and . . . every living thing that moveth upon the earth." This predisposition likely owes to a certain set of genes on the Y chromosome that, as in the case of the Marx Brothers, not to mention the Three Stooges, have a natural tendency to feed off each other. Chief amongst them, it would appear, is what we might call the "War Gene." Just how influential is the "War Gene" on male behavior?

- Name one corporation that does not perceive itself as being "at war" with its competitors; that does not want to "destroy" its competitors
- Name one videogame that is not based on war
- Name one team-sport that is not based on war
- Name one summer movie that is not based on war
- Name one men's action-novel that is not based on war
- Name one male-child play-fantasy that is not based on war
- Name one government eradication project that is not a war on something or other
- Name one street gang that does not perceive itself as being "at war" with its rivals

61
Boys Must Be Boys

MALE CHILDREN ARE NO SOONER ABLE TO HOLD OBJECTS IN their hands, and make percussive sounds with their lips, than they are locked in fierce battles with all manner of villains and evil-doers. If their well-meaning parents should refuse to give their little angels a toy version of the traditional instruments of war, those same little angels will soon enough invent their own. Alas, what common (if slightly crooked) stick is not a light-saber, or a SEAL team assault rifle? What Legos building block is not a grenade, or a bomb?

Evolutionary biology suggests that human males are the way they are because natural selection made them so. And natural section made them so because a certain combination of physical strength, aggressiveness, pigheadedness, daringdoness, and emotional stuntedness is what has allowed our species to survive for 400,000 years.

In other words, the human male's predisposition toward aggression and destruction had its uses, and was sufficiently controllable by the community at large, as well as by the natural limitations of scale, that the catastrophic damage we are witnessing today, to "every living thing," was simply not possible in earlier epochs, when there were relatively few of our kind around.

The question now is: Does the male behavior of yore, as expressed by the War Gene and its many kissing cousins, including the Get Even Gene and the Blow Stuff Up Gene, have the same practical utility today it had 400 millennia ago? Or has it become an anachronism, and a very dangerous one at that? What do we see in this regard when we take a step back and look at the state of our world today?

62
Man Made

C IVILIZATION AS WE KNOW IT WAS IMAGINED AND CONSTRUCTED largely by males.

Arks and supertankers, lynching ropes and gas chambers, cave drawings and renaissance paintings, hovels and skyscrapers, kites and jets, Olympian gods and celestial monarchs, arithmetic and calculus, battering rams and ballistic missiles, on and on, are almost exclusively artifacts of—indeed, reflections of—the male psyche.

In other words, most of what we experience as civilization is "man" made. Which begs the question: What might the world look like today if it had been imagined and constructed over the millennia by men and women in roughly equal measure?

Can we know this? To be sure, we cannot know it in any detail. However, we can at least speculate, here and there, on the basis of our understanding of how the female psyche fundamentally differs from its male counterpart. Take, for example, the institution of the Catholic Church. If the female psyche had been allowed to be as influential in the Catholic Church's founding and development over the past 2000+ years as has been the male psyche,

- Would the Church be as hierarchal as it is today?
- As dogmatic and rule-bound?
- As judgmental?
- As exclusionary?
- As inflexible?
- As misogynous?
- As homophobic

Alas, what if women alone, instead of men alone, had invented religion? How many tomes of rules and dogma would have been amassed over the centuries? How much convoluted theology would have been invented? How many excommunications would there have been? How many Inquisitions? How many burnings at the stake? How many calls for eternal damnation?

63
Yin & Yang

N HIS FAMOUS *Autobiography*, BEN FRANKLIN PROFFERS THE FOLLOWING 13 virtues as "necessary or desirable:"

Industry	Justice
Frugality	Moderation
Order	Cleanliness
Resolution	Tranquility
Temperance	Chastity
Silence	Humility
Sincerity	

He does not explicitly tell us "necessary or desirable" toward what end, but it is apparent from context he means "necessary or desirable' toward achieving material success. Indeed, what is the aim of Industry and Frugality, either alone or in concert, if not to maintain a full larder?

If Franklin had, in his time, been a little more in touch with his yin self relative to his yang self, he might have noticed a need for a second set of virtues, to complement the first set. Indeed, whereas Ben's virtues collectively stand in service to one's own interests (are inward-focused), the missing virtues would collectively stand in service to one's neighbor's interests (be outward-focused). These complementing virtues might aptly be called the 13 relational virtues, and might include the following or the like:

Compassion	Forbearance
Empathy	Nurturance
Forgiveness	Fairness
Sacrifice	Loyalty
Reverence	Tolerance
Generosity	Trust
Contrition	

QUESTION: What if Franklin had mentioned the latter virtues in his *Autobiography*? What if he had given them equal weight relative to his 13 inward-focused virtues? How might the world have turned out differently?

64

Where's Rachel When You *Really* Need Her?

THE FOLLOWING EXCERPT WAS TAKEN FROM AN ARTICLE commemorating the 50th anniversary of the publication of Rachel Carson's *Silent Spring* ("Calm Leadership, Lasting Change, by Nancy F. Koehn, *New York Times*, October 28, 2012):

"She was a slight, soft-spoken woman who preferred walking the Maine shoreline to stalking the corridors of power. And yet Rachel Carson, the author of *Silent Spring*, played a central role in starting the environmental movement, by forcing government and business [a.k.a. the male establishment] to confront the dangers of pesticides.

"Carson was a scientist with a lyrical bent who saw it as her mission to share her observations with a wider audience. In the course of her work, she also felt called upon to become a leader—and was no less powerful for being a reluctant one."

QUESTION: How might we get the Rachel Carson's of the modern world to overcome what would appear to be a continuing reluctance on their part to pursue or accept leadership roles? Or is this reluctance simply un-overcomeable in the large? Rachel Carson, after all, had no children to shepherd or husband to defer to.

65

The Blue States of America

CONSIDERING THE DEEP DIVIDES THAT EXIST TODAY BETWEEN THE Blue States and the Red States, might it be time for the former to separate from the latter? If so, might the following principles be used to knit the Blue States into an alternative union?

1. Every citizen benefits from every other citizen being educated and/or trained to the extent possible.

2. Every citizen has as many undeniable responsibilities as inalienable rights.

3. No individual or group of individuals holds or can hold a superior level of authority over the right of a woman to exercise dominion over her own body.

4. Every truth, right, principle, and original intention is subject to interpretation.

5. Human kind has a moral duty to respect, steward, and conserve the natural world.

6. Every citizen has a right to access some minimal level of healthcare.

7. Every citizen has an obligation to maintain his or her health toward minimizing the need for (expensive) medical interventions, especially in later life.

8. Citizenship requires of every citizen some minimal amount of public service.

9. Religion is a private matter and has no standing in the realm of governance.

10. We need not love our neighbors but we have a moral obligation to look after them.

11. A complex world requires a proportionate amount of regulation.

12 Terminating a life as punishment for a crime, however heinous, is a form of barbarism.

13. All public policy should be informed by three goals: The well-being of the family; the protection of women and girls; the socialization of boys.

If the Blue States were to declare independence from the Red States, would there be a war; or would there be a great sigh of relief . . . from all concerned?

66
Panel of Our Peers

O UR SYSTEM OF JUSTICE IS BASED ON THE THEORY THAT WE HAVE a fundamental right to be judged by a panel of our peers versus by the king's (or state's) representatives. To field a panel of our peers, we use random selection (conscription). (Once upon a time, we employed this same technique to field an army of citizen-soldiers.)

What if our system of governance were similarly based? What if, at all levels, our personal and collective interests were represented not by self-interested, eminently-corruptible politicians, always seeking personal advantage, but by average citizens selected by lot?

What if there were no career politicians? No negative campaign ads? No endless electioneering? No gerrymandering. No entrenched partisanship. No shameless dissembling? No political robo-calls? No PACs? No pundits? No Donald Trumps?

What if our entire culture were constructed around the notion that every citizen, however humble in his or her abilities or achievements, was subject to conscription into public service, just as every (male) citizen was, once upon a time, subject to conscription into a common defense? Indeed, isn't this what a democracy *really* is?

67

Lincoln: Man of Principle or Just Another Pol?

In a letter published in the New York Tribune *on August 22, 1862, President Lincoln declared that his "paramount object in the struggle [Civil War] is to save the Union, and is not either to save or destroy slavery." In fact, Lincoln did not enact the Emancipation Proclamation until January 1, 1863, two years after the Civil War had begun.*

So why was Lincoln so hell-bent on preserving the Union, and so equivocal about ending "the moral, social, and political evil of slavery [Lincoln's words]?"

Short answer: Money.

Slightly longer answer: The economic survival of the North.

The North had the textile mills and the water power to run them, but it did not have the cotton. The South had the cotton, not to mention the slaves to plant, grow, and harvest it. If the South were to leave the union, Lincoln well knew, the North would no longer be able to rely on the South's cotton to supply its mills. In fact, worse case, the South could rely entirely on Great Britain to buy its cotton, and thereby leave the North out of the cotton-textile equation altogether.

In regard to his reluctance to end "the moral, social, and political evil of slavery," Lincoln was keenly aware that if, at war's end, the labor for planting, growing, and harvesting Southern were no longer free, the price of cotton would jump on the open market and once again the economic survival of the North would be in jeopardy.

Alas, isn't it <u>always</u> about the money?

68
On Building
a Better Mousetrap

THE DISTRIBUTION OF MOST HUMAN TRAITS CAN BE REPRESENTED by a bell curve, where the two ends of the curve represent the extreme occurrences of a particular trait, and the summit of the curve represents the mean between the extremes.

Take, for example, the distribution of height in the adult male. We would expect the far-left potion of the curve for this trait to indicate a relative infrequency of small-statured males; the far-right portion to indicate a relative infrequency of large-statured males. Visually, it would be easy to see that the proportion of adult males who are either extremely small-statured or extremely large-statured is relatively small. A similar curve would apply, presumably, to male aggressiveness, with a small percentage of males manifesting as Ferdinand the Bulls; an equally small percentage manifesting as Attila the Huns. In fact, aren't such relative extremes central to our survival over millennia? Isn't it at the extremes of any particular trait, in fact, where nature tinkers most boldly toward building a better mousetrap? And aren't we all, our race as a whole, the result of this bold tinkering? To the tinkerers goes the future?

69
Declaration 2.0

WE THE PEOPLE OF THE BLUE STATES OF AMERICA, IN SEEKING TO form a mutually beneficial affiliation, are prepared to take all necessary measures, save the taking up of arms, to remove ourselves from the reach and peril of the following tyrannies:

- The Tyranny of Ignorance
- The Tyranny of Arrogance
- The Tyranny of Intolerance
- The Tyranny of Superstition
- The Tyranny of Self-Righteousness
- The Tyranny of Closed-Mindedness
- The Tyranny of Expediency
- The Tyranny of Ideology
- The Tyranny of Zealotry
- The Tyranny of Rigidity
- The Tyranny of Extremism
- The Tyranny of Absolutism
- The Tyranny of Obstructionism

We hold these tyrannies to be counterproductive to all individual and collective pursuits of happiness. We will not countenance their intrusion into our lives, nor abide any individual or group of individuals who would, of a poverty of humility, or an extravagance of self-certainty, inflict them upon us.

Meat'n'Taters

1

On "Draining the Swamp"

B<small>Y ALL ACCOUNTS, OUR PRESENT SYSTEM OF GOVERNANCE—</small> wherein the citizenry elects third parties (politicians) to represent its interests—is failing. As a result, a host of problems— faltering schools, crumbling infrastructure, pandemic opioid abuse, surging violence, rapidly-changing climate, accelerating inequality, burgeoning political intransigence et al—are not being addressed in a timely and effectual manner.

The primary culprit here would appear to be the fact that the politicians we elect to represent our interests do not, in large measure, perform this quasi-sacred function. Instead, they allow themselves to be co-opted by moneyed interests (oligarchs) who contribute large sums of money to politicians' re-election campaigns in exchange for present and / or future "considerations."

Another likely culprit is an ever-increasing amount of disaffection among the citizenry—emanant from ever-greater amounts of apathy and cynicism—leading to ever-greater numbers of citizens giving up on government altogether. Government, they conclude, is corrupt and ineffectual by its very nature—always has been, always will be—so why bother? Why set one's self up for one disappointment after another by harboring hope that, by golly, this time around our "leaders" will do the right thing?

Unfortunately, doing what would be necessary to ensure ourselves of a government that didn't create more problems than it solved would likely involve making fundamental changes to our Constitution and system of government, including replacing our election-based system with a conscription-based system similar to the one used by our system of justice to field panels of jurors.

Thinking the Unthinkable

For many of us, though, perhaps most of us, messing with the Constitution in a fundamental way is unthinkable. There are several reasons for this, including the fact that many Americans consider the U. S. Constitution to be a sacred document, on par with Judeo-Christian scripture, and therefore off-limits to undergoing fundamental change. Others of us, although unpersuaded by the sacred-document argument, nevertheless hold a similar view; namely that the Constitution was conceived in a unique moment in human history that could not possibly be replicated.

Both of these views are reflected in the title of a seminal history of the Constitutional Convention of 1787, namely Catherine Drinker Bowen's *Miracle at Philadelphia*.

Another factor weighing against making fundamental changes to the Constitution is humankind's inherent tendency to keep the devil they know versus opting for one they don't.

Finally, concerning conscription specifically, there is the unthinkability of placing real power and real authority into the hands of, not only average blokes but sub-average blokes as well, the latter consisting, at least in part, of those invisible throngs Hillary Clinton (in)famously dismissed as "deplorables." And yet, as alluded to above, our entire system of justice has, for the past 225 years, been based on exactly the concept being floated here toward making the unthinkable not only thinkable but inevitable.

The Mass of Men

Unfortunately, many of us not habitually in communication with the great "mass of men" tend to hold the entire lot in low esteem, taking as our cue perhaps the manifest misanthropy of the perpetrator of the Great Flood. We much prefer not to swim in the same pool with them, and even more emphatically, we much prefer not to be represented by them. In the same way we don't trust their hygiene, we don't trust their capacity for sophisticated thinking and / or dealing with complex or subtle issues.

Are we not required to ask, though, why it is we can trust these same Janes and Joes to function effectively in our system of justice, but cannot trust them to function effectively in our system of governance? Do not the people involved in both cases need to analyze mounds of oft-conflicting evidence, make reasoned judgments on the basis of this evidence, and take moral responsibility for the judgments they make?

In fact, do not all human beings crave trust and responsibility (a.k.a. respect) as a matter of genetic imperative? If given the opportunity, will they not more often than not rise to the occasion? Do we not see this, in fact, across the spectrum of human endeavor? Take Corporate America, for example. Do not those corporations that treat their employees like children tend to get exactly what they expect, untrustworthy employees, whereas those corporations that treat their employees like adults tend to get exactly what they expect, loyal employees? Is it not true, in fact, that very few Janes or Joes—alas, even very few "deplorables"—would deliberately abuse a vested trust, or treat a weighty responsibility lightly?

Alas, "draining the swamp"—a.k.a. ridding governance of the effluvia despoiling it—is an alluring notion. The problem is, unless structural changes are made at the same time, will not the same ol' bog fill up again with the same ol' sludge?

2
Parable
of Ed and Henry

[From Poor Richard's Lament *by Tom Fitzgerald.*
Prescott Bahr, a former crack addict, is attempting to inspire a recovering
addict who has been clean for a week but is terrified of backsliding.]

PRESCOTT SAT BACK [IN HIS CHAIR]. "OK, THIS STORY CONCERNS TWO dudes who, like you, attended NA meetings every day in their first week on the clean cart. Unlike you, though, one of them attended only morning meetings; the other only evening meetings. On the seventh day for each, the first dude, let's call him Ed, attended his usual morning meeting, and after being congratulated by his meeting mates, he set out for home with a bright blue ribbon pinned to his chest, feeling pretty good about himself. After walking about a block or so, he was approached by a little girl dressed in rags who held a daffodil in one hand and a crisp one-hundred-dollar bill in the other. 'Take one,' she said to Ed, 'and leave the other behind.'

"Now, being a wily, street-savvy dude, Ed was a little suspicious at first, but a quick look around for obvious signs of a setup put his mind at ease, and so he took the hundred-dollar bill from the little girl, examined it for signs of counterfeiting, and stuffed it in his pocket. He walked on feeling like he had just won the lottery, and soon came to a corner where a tout named Tom was slinging his wares."

Roddy grinned. "This must be a true story, 'cause I knows ol' Tom real well."

Prescott smiled. "Ed knew ol' Tom real well too, and ol' Tom knew Ed, and in no time at all, good ol' Tom had good ol' Ed all fixed up with the best rock money can buy. What the hell, Ed told himself.

"He deserved it. He'd gotten himself through a whole week clean and sober, and he had just won the lottery! It was time to party! So Ed continued on, in a party mood, and after sauntering a block or so further on, came upon an old derelict druggie named Fat Annie, for her swollen arms and legs, who had tried to go straight more times than she could begin to remember. Ed greeted Annie by showing her his blue-tipped vials, invited her to his party, and needless to say, was never seen at morning meeting again."

Roddy shook his head.

"OK, now, the other dude in our story, let's call him Henry, also attended a meeting on the seventh day, in the evening; was also praised by his mates for making it through a whole week; and was also given a bright blue ribbon to wear on his chest. And after walking about a block or so after his meeting, he too was approached by a little ragamuffin holding a single daffodil in one hand and a crisp one-hundred-dollar bill in the other. Take one,' she said to Henry, 'and leave the other behind.'

"Noticing the girl's rags and unwashed hair, Henry removed the ribbon from his nice clean shirt, pinned it to the little girl's grimy blouse, and left her with the hundred-dollar bill. Continuing on, he soon came to the corner where ol' Tom was slinging his wares.

"Recognizing Henry, Tom offered him the best rock money can buy, and, just for him, at a special price. To which offer, Henry held up the daffodil and said, 'How many hits for this lovely flower, Tom?'

"To which query, ol' Tom turned his attention to a more promising prospect, and Henry continued on his way, soon happening upon an old derelict druggie named Fat Annie. Smiling into Annie's bloodshot eyes, Henry offered her the daffodil and said, 'For you, Annie. For all the times you tried.'

"Taking the flower into a trembling hand, Annie wept, and said back, 'No one's ever given me a flower before.'

"To which lament, Henry replied, 'The error was theirs, dear Annie, not yours,' and then, with a nod, he walked on.

"The following day, when Henry arrived at evening meeting, he noticed a new person in attendance, sitting in the back row, and sat down beside her. Saying not a word, he reached over and, taking hold of Fat Annie's swollen hand, gave it a squeeze."

Roddy's eyes filled.

"Ed is the person I used to be, Roddy, and could be again"—Prescott snapped his fingers—"just like that. Henry is the person I had to become in order to keep Ed from rearing his ugly head every time some little thing went wrong. Ed I can become without any effort at all. Ed is always willing. Henry I can become, or be, only by choice. Moment to moment. Step by step."

3

Parable
of the Cosmic Seafarer

[From Poor Richard's Lament *by Tom Fitzgerald.*
Ben Franklin, returned to Earth for a day, is about to address a leadership
conference in the Grand Ballroom at the Waldorf Astoria in New York.
He has been mistaken as a spontaneous entertainment.]

TAKING A DEEP BREATH, BEN BEGAN: "THOUGH THE HOUR IS DEAR, yet still there is time."

Ben held silent a moment, and then continued. "Many years ago now, during the course of a leisurely chess match, my opponent, the sister of a notable admiral and an equally notable general, told me a story that, at the time, I surmised a ploy toward distraction.

"It had been told her, she avowed, showing a certain affect of eye, whilst holding her queen's rook betwixt two fingers, by a serpent in her garden. It bears, I hope you might agree, repeating."

Nary a sound.

"Not so very long ago, a great seafarer, greatly troubled by the course of events in his native world, this being called by us Mars, after the Roman god of war—'god of war,' good people—set out in his brigantine to sail the great seas of Mars, in company with himself alone, in search of a great leader. His earnest intention was to prevail upon this leader to save his people from a fate most dire, they having abandoned their sextants and compasses, of their own free will, such as to follow a sundry of pipers and sirens unto a ready fulfillment of every desire. He first sought out a great leader of state, he ensconced in a great white castle, and asked of him, 'Good sir, for whom would you forfeit your office and all your powers such that they, each one, might have opportunity sufficient?' Whereupon the great leader of state consulted his timepiece and declared himself tardy for a ceremony of high importance. Next, our seafarer sought out a great leader of commerce, he ensconced in a castle of glass and steel, and asked of him, 'Good sir, for whom would you forfeit your office and all your riches such that they, each one, might have means enough?' Whereupon the great leader of commerce consulted his timepiece and declared himself tardy for a meeting of high importance. Next, our seafarer sought out a great leader of religion, he ensconced in a great castle of fresco and gilt, and asked of him: 'Good sir, for whom would you forfeit your office and place in heaven such that they, each one, might have hope enough?'

"Whereupon the great leader of religion looked to his timepiece and declared himself tardy for a ritual of high importance. And so it went, from sea to sea, continent to continent, isle to isle, until our seafarer had exhausted all possibility."

Nary a sound.

"Discouraged but undiminished of resolve, our seafarer fitted his brigantine for navigating the great aether, and embarked then, to a fair solar wind, for a nearby world, the one known to us as Venus. At no greater than halfway to this other world, however, our intrepid seafarer happened into a great cosmic storm and, blown off course by unrelenting gales of negative seeking after positive, positive seeking after negative, was carried instead to the world we know as Earth, there coming to rest upon a great shoal of rock. Dropping his anchor into a rocky crag, in caution against tides unknown, our seafarer took to his glass and soon espied a man, very strange in appearance, sitting upon a nearby ledge, his face uplifted toward the sun. This strange apparition had very long hair, purely white, an even longer beard, also white, and was wearing a robe as purely white as his beard and hair. Even stranger still, this man appeared to have only two eyes as against three, and only two arms as against six, and he showed no purple of complexion soever."

Nary a sound.

"Buoyed now by a flood-tide of hope, our seafarer launched his pinnace and rowed through gentle currents of air—whilst a great winged creature, white of crown and wingtip, yellow of beak and eye, soared in proximity—to whereat the bearded man was seated.

"Tethering his pinnace to a gnarled shrub rooted in a small fissure, our seafarer approached the bearded man, and clearing his throat, such as to gain the strange man's attention, said unto him, 'Take me unto your leader, good sir, if you would be so kind.' "

Murmurs of amusement.

"The bearded man stared at his curious visitor, purple of complexion, bearing not two eyes but three, not two arms but six, and gave the only reply he might: 'I cannot, sir, for there is none such to be found here, whether I should pilot you to north or to south, to east or to west.'

"To this declaration, our seafarer slumped as if to loose a burden he could no longer bear.

" 'If it were an Egoist you sought, sir,' the bearded man continued, 'or a Narcissist, or a Self-Aggrandizer, there are bazaars innumerable, north and south, east and west, to which I might direct you.

" 'If it were a Demagogue you desired, sir, or a Chauvinist, or a Populist, there are flesh houses inexhaustible, north and south, east and west, to which I might direct you.

" 'If it were an Ideologue you required, sir, or a Zealot, or a Dogmatist, there are carnivals aplenty, north and south, east and west, to which I might direct you.

" 'But a leader?' He shook his head most severely. 'I fear, sir, you have traveled a very long way to no avail soever.'

"One great weight compounded by another, the latter being fatigue, our seafarer inquired of the bearded man if he might tarry with him for a spell in repose, sufficient that he might recover his strength, thereby his resolve, before resuming his journey.

" 'Rest for as long as you require,' the bearded man replied, 'or longer still. You are most welcome here. Be cautioned, however, that this small shelf is affixed to an earthly bowel much disposed toward fits of colic.'

"Our seafarer sat down, releasing a deep sigh, and inquired of his host by what name he should be addressed.

" 'I have no name,' the bearded man replied. 'In one time and place, I was called The Awakened; in another, The Wise; in another, The Prophet. Now, I am called by no name at all, by no man at all.'

" 'Should I not call you Teacher then, in keeping with what your very nature would seem to name you?'

"Thereupon the man of no name directed toward our seafarer a scowl most severe. 'You should not. What I was by natural inclination of heart and spirit, I did not, to my eternal regret, become by will and resolve.'

"Our seafarer looked away for a moment, marveling at the aerial grace of the great winged creature he had earlier espied, it gliding nearby, then looked again to the man of no name. 'Should I infer then, sir, that if you were to be granted means to travel backward in time, and have opportunity thereby to correct all your errata, or any selection thereof, you would invite Will and Resolve to power your wagon?'

" 'I would do precisely that.'

" 'Leading it thereupon to where, sir, if I might inquire?'

" 'Aught else but to this airy prison.'

" 'And just how was it, if I might inquire, sir, that you came to take residence here?'

"The man of no name looked down upon his crossed legs—he being seated in the Indian manner—then, taking a deep breath, cleared his throat. 'I was banished to this igneous shelf for having committed the most egregious of all earthly sins: to wit, speaking that which is not to be heard, challenging that which is not to be questioned, accusing those who are not to be reproached. I had become much alarmed, you see, too alarmed to remain passive, thereby acquiescent, over a proliferation of penny pipers playing false anthems throughout the land, to effect indeed of equating pleasure with happiness, desire with need, acquisition with success, satiation with fulfillment, self with center. By inclination of heart—certainly not that of good sense—I made attempt toward some measure of dissent. I carried a small box onto a public Common, and standing upon this pulpit, sang out, "The true leader promotes, by example, not appetite but need; not acquisition but contribution, not satiation but fulfillment; not profit but succor." Before I might draw a breath such as to continue, I was removed from my trespass by bludgeons of scorn and derision. Bruised of feeling, but undaunted of spirit, I carried my box to a second Common and there sang out: "The true leader does not crave power, but is embarrassed by it, does not run for office, but from it." Before I might repeat myself, however, in the cause of reinforcement, I was removed from my trespass by fusillades of brick and stone. Bruised of body but undaunted still, I carried my box to a third Common and there sang out: "The true leader dwells not in a great domed palace, serviced by eunuchs, but with his flock, bearing in tempest and peril all that they must bear." I was thereupon set upon by a mob of Knights of the One True Way, pummeled to the very threshold of a blessed death, and brought before the Supreme Directorate for the Propagation of Proper Thinking, which body declared me, prima facie, a minion of the Unholy One and banished me to wherefrom no man might call me forth. I was carried here by the very raptor you see soaring and gliding about this lonely platform, keeping always one yellow eye upon me.'

"Animated now as if by stroke of electrical flux, our seafarer cried out, ''Tis you! 'Tis you I seek!' He thereupon explained, in a single semantic unit, unbroken by any mark soever, the purpose of his mission, and the cause of its urgency. When finally he had finished, the man of no name, who had listened in a grudging silence, replied, most vehemently: 'I am no such thing!' He pulled at his beard as if at a cord to summon the sergeant-at-arms. 'Besides which,' he added, 'we are of wholly different worlds, you and I.'

"Our seafarer smiled in a knowing sort of way, being cautious, however, not to tread unto smugness. 'I am a great seafarer, sir. I have been to most every place there is to go, and I can tell you, sir, with a confidence rivaling your resistance, that there is no such thing as separate worlds. The line of demarcation with which mortal beings separate one thing from another, one self from another, one world from another, is but a construct of convenience, with no basis in fact. We declare separation but where expediency invites, such as to accommodate ownership, hence avarice; such as to accommodate hierarchy, hence dominion; such as to accommodate boundary, hence difference. True, you are not purplish, as I; but is it coloration that marks the true leader, sir, or is it something deeper? True, you have only two eyes as against three, as I; but is it acuity of sight that marks the true leader, sir, or is it something far keener? True, you have but two arms as against six, as I; but is it agility of limb that marks the true leader, sir, or is it something far more facile?'

"Feeling in the moment a violent quaking of the earth, and hearing a deep rumbling, our seafarer looked up to discover a large boulder hurtling down the declination of the mount, directly toward the ledge upon which he and the man of no name were seated; and in that instant, he sprang to upright, as if indeed of mere reflex, and grasping the man of no name by facility of six arms in simultaneity, tossed him, without benefit of ceremony, into the safety of the pinnace, taking thereupon the falling rock fully onto himself.

"On the world known to us as Mars, named after the Roman god of war—'god of war,' good people—a man named Argaa opened his eyes, all three in the instant, and discovered himself in his comfortable bed, within his humble abode, which stood at the edge of the great sea Lauraa, within the shadow of the great volcano Tomaasio.

"In the moment, Argaa knew what it was he must needs do, could no longer decline from doing, to whatever excuse. And in this moment he felt most keenly not that blessed relief that attends upon escaping an imagined horror, but a most profound sense of grief, for his very life, he knew, was forfeit.

" 'Check, and mate,' my wily opponent said unto me, in way of concluding her story.

" 'Ah, I see I am beaten,' I lamented.

" 'Is not such a condition known but to Pride?' she replied.

" 'Ah, so it is,' I said. 'So it is.' "

Ben peered up at the chandelier of six globes surrounding one lower, and thereupon looked upon the three battalions of militia arrayed before him. "Several are the measures of the true leader.

"Three such, however, I submit, should precede all others. In the form of interrogatives, asked of one's own self, they are thus:

"For what causes would I, without benefit of forethought, forfeit my very life, that these causes might succeed?

"For what principles would I, without benefit of forethought, forfeit my very life, that these principles might prevail?

"For what persons would I, without benefit of forethought, forfeit my very life, that these persons might continue in theirs?"

Ben counted as if six tolls of bell, and then looked to Mr. Dunleavy.

"I do hope my remarks were appropriate to the occasion, sir. I yield to the speaker who would be the president of your nation, such that he might commerce remarks too long delayed by a foolish old man."

4

Parable
of the Seven Hapless Victims

[From Poor Richard's Lament *by Tom Fitzgerald.
Ben Franklin, returned to Earth for a day, is about the address
the guest diners at a church-housed soup kitchen in New York.]*

C LIMBING NOW ONTO THE RAISED PLATFORM, THIS SHOWING THE same checkerboard pattern, black squares alternating with white, as encountered in the corridor at the Waldorf Astoria, Ben turned half-circle around, such as to face upon the archipelago of tables.

"It would appear to be a general law of nature," he began, his voice only slightly elevated, for lack of strength to raise it farther, "that in every group of at least seven persons, there is at least one leader." He paused, allowing a modest clattering emanant from the ancillary building to become the only fissure upon an eggshell of silence. In the interim, he noticed a Negro man, light of skin, peering upon him from nearby the entry to the ancillary building. The man's dress and deportment suggested authority; his phrenology, Jamaica; his eyes, equanimity.

The man nodding, Ben returned the gesture in kind, and then continued. "It would appear to be a general law of nature, good friends, that in every accidental assemblage of at least seven persons, there is included amongst them at least one natural leader—as indeed was the case in ancient China, in the year 4004 BC, when, according to Chu Fung Ming, the great chronicler, seven wayfarers discovered themselves one moonless night fallen into the same pit, at the bottom of which was a well filled to brim. Their prison being absent any purchase for ascendance, their fate would appear to be absent all hope.

"At first, there was much despairing amongst the seven, and not a little self-pitying, but then, come morning, one of the seven, ciphering by eye the height of the pit, and gaining the attention thereupon of his six companions, this by way of breaking into song—'If I had a hammer / I'd hammer in the morning / I'd hammer in the evening . . .'—said unto his comrades: 'Fellow travelers, if we are to stand here as individuals, alone in our despair, passive in our helplessness, dispirited in our sorrow, here we shall remain; here we shall perish, none of us having yet fully lived. If, however, we were to agree to decide, by simple lottery, who amongst us should be escaped by the other six, we might then construct a ladder of ourselves, each man, save the bottom-most, sitting upon the shoulders of another, such that the highest-most might then stand to full height upon the shoulders of the second-highest man, and thereupon pull himself unto liberation.'

"All agreeing to this scheme, our seven accidental victims proceeded to draw lots, each knowing that only one of their number would be escaped, but that, even so, the six left behind would have helped a fellow traveler gain a second chance at living his life to fullest. Now, as fate would farther have it for our seven star-crossed travelers, the leader of this scheme, although drawing lastly, drew the numeral 1, thereby entitling him, by assumption of the six others, to first choice regarding claiming a position upon the human ladder. Immediately thereupon, there was much grumbling and dissension amongst the six losers, this devolving unto accusation and recrimination, our unhappy six having previously learnt, by way of much travail, to suspicion the intentions of any but themselves alone. Our leader, however, being in fact a true leader, responded in the only way such a one might, saying unto his companions: 'O no, no, you misunderstand. I thought I had been clear: The person drawing the numeral 1 is to stand in the first position, that is, at bottom, whilst the person drawing the numeral 7 is to stand in the seventh position, that is, at top.' And with this declaration, the other six travelers freely assented to their chosen lots.

"And so a human ladder was constructed of our seven travelers, the sixth bearing upward the seventh upon his shoulders; the fifth bearing upward these two upon his shoulders; and so on and so on until the first man, our leader, was bearing upon his shoulders, at bottom, more weight than any man should ever be expected or allowed.

"Steadied then by the uplifted arms of the sixth man, our seventh traveler raised himself to full height and, reaching upward, managed to grasp sufficient purchase beyond the rim of the pit as to be able to pull himself unto freedom, leaving thereby his fellow travelers behind— which condition, our escaped traveler at once realized, he simply could not abide. Indeed, the six fellows left behind, only recently but strangers to him, were now his brethren. Either all seven were to thrive together, or all seven were to perish together— and that was an end on it!

"In this moment of realization, something very strange occurred:

"Where, in the far recesses of this traveler's imagination, there heretofore had been little evidence of natural cunning or creative facility, there now emerged, like a genie from a lantern long unattended, a most vivid image, which image our escaped traveler immediately strove to imitate. Firstly, he implored his comrades to bear yet a little longer the burden the draw of lots had fated upon each one.

"He then set about renting his shirt and breeches into ribbons, and weaving these into a strand of sturdy cord. Upon finishing his work, he lowered one end to this cord to the sixth traveler, such as to be able to pull his brother also unto liberation.

"Now, as you might have anticipated, upon his being escaped by this collaborative means, our sixth traveler converted his own clothing into a strand of cord, which article he added to the first, such so that he and his comrade could thereupon pull the fifth traveler unto freedom. And so it went until all seven comrades were escaped, and standing in each other's company, as starkly and joyfully naked, except for the last comrade, as babes new born."

Looking to Alice, Ben discovered her partly obstructed from view by an attendant, who, removing something from pocket, gave this over to Alice. Looking to the Jamaican gentleman, who nodded, Ben nodded in return, and then continued. "As most of you can well affirm, I suspicion, pain tends to shorten the range of one's vision. The greater the agony, the shorter the range. Consider the miller whose hand has become entrapped under a grinding stone.

"How far beyond the wall of his agony might this poor fellow, in the moment, cast his eyes?

"Indeed, the more pain we suffer, of whatever species, emanate of whatever source, the more likely we are to miss observing that, no matter how wretched might be our present circumstance, no matter how deep might be the pit into which we have tumbled, we are never alone. Always there are like-others in close proximity, indeed not more than an arm's length away. In this regard, you might wish to take notice in the moment that you are presently in company with, in most cases, at least six like-others; and farther, that the lot of you are arranged as you would be were you sitting at the bottom of a pit containing a well; and farther, that there is no immediate cause for you to leave the company of your tablemates until such time as one amongst you has ventured to stand and sing a few notes of a worthy ode."

Ben held now to silence, the only sound being a muted clattering emanate from the ancillary building. The Jamaican gentleman appeared as if not breathing. The milk and rose attendants among the tables were wholly hesitated from rendering farther service.

Of a sudden Alice Kortright upstood at her table: "If I had a hammer / I'd hammer in the morning / I'd hammer in the evening—"

A gentleman rose at a table just forward and rightward of where Ben was standing—"I'd hammer out danger / I'd hammer out a warning—"

A gentleman rose at a third table—"I'd hammer out love between my brothers and my sisters / all over this land."

Another woman rose at Alice's table.

And so on—and so on—

Upon nodding unto the Jamaican gentleman, the gentleman nodding in return, Ben descended from the altar. Making his way then toward the baptismal, he came upon Alice, she yet upstanding, and discovered her holding in hand a lavender bloom, upright, like a candle. Affixed to the stem was a bright-green ribbon upon which something had been writ, there being two letters visible toward the terminus of one tail: V-E.

The other of Alice's hair ribbons, Ben noticed, was affixed upon the stem of bloom in the hand of the woman to rightward, she being also upstanding, and also singing.

"I'd ring it in the evening / all over this land / I'd ring out danger / I'd ring out a warning / I'd ring out love between my brothers and my sisters / all over this land . . ."

Thereupon tapping his way into the vestibule, Ben paused there, and turning half-circle around, faced upon the chancel.

Well we've got a hammer
And we've got a bell
And we've got a song to sing
All over this land
It's the hammer of justice
It's the bell of freedom
It's the song about love between my brothers and my sisters
All over this land

Taking his leave with a bow, Ben tapped his way from the church . . .

5
Ben Franklin's Big Mistake

[Some of the material in this essay appears previously in this volume.]

THINGS DON'T SEEM TO BE GOING VERY WELL IN AMERICA THESE days. Our national debt is historic, our government is in paralysis, our schools are in crisis, our popular culture is daily reaching new lows in coarseness and superficiality. Greed, narcissism, rudeness, and a smug ignorance abound. Obesity is epidemic. Instability and angst pervade every dimension of public and private life. Why?

Does this troubling reality represent an inevitability—a generalized decline dictated by some immutable law of history—or is something else going on? There are, predictably, an abundance of opinions on the matter, but there can be only one truth. In pursuit of this truth, this essay, drawing from *Poor Richard's Lament*, conjectures an unexpected root cause for our woes, and thereby an equally unexpected course of redemption.

Part 1: Something Rotten in Denmark

In *Poor Richard's Lament*, Ben Franklin has been confined to a private apartment in purgatory since his death in 1790. He's supposed to have been contemplating his "errata," but instead has added twelve more volumes to his *Autobiography*. Having, over the years, grown ever more impatient with his situation, Ben has several times over petitioned the celestial bureaucracy for final disposition of his case.

Finally, he has been granted his day in court.

In the first half of *Poor Richard's Lament*, Ben is examined in the Celestial Court of Petitions by three former enemies, including John Adams. By the end of his examination, which forces Ben to confront things about his past he has steadfastly been avoiding—including his participation in the commerce and convenience of slavery, and his cruel treatment of his family—Ben expects to be cast into the Abyss.

Instead, he is invited to return to Earth to bear witness to what has become of his "Dear Country" in the two and a quarter centuries of his absence.

In the second half of *Poor Richard's Lament*, Ben begins his odyssey of witness on Milk Street in Boston, where he was born; passes through New York, where he crashes a leadership conference at the Waldorf Astoria; and eventually makes his way to his grave site at Christ Church burying ground in Philadelphia.

In passing through Boston Common, Ben finds a newspaper on a park bench and, of course, cannot resist. What better way to take the measure of a generation, after all, than to gather in the news of the day.

Here are some of the news items Ben gathers in:

1. A man had been arrested in Atlanta, Ga., for sending an explosive device disguised as a cell phone to the CEO of Global Tel. The device had failed to go off when the package was opened. The man claimed he had not intended for the device to go off; he simply wanted to get someone in authority at the company to pay attention to his complaints, which he had registered several times, by various means, including certified mail, to no effect. The CEO of Global Tel, D. Sanger Bornstein, recently received a performance bonus valued at $35.5 million.

2. A Catholic bishop had resigned from office after being charged with leaving the scene of a fatal accident. The same bishop had recently struck a deal with prosecutors to avoid indictment for protecting priests accused of child molestation. The elderly woman struck by the bishop had died at the scene.

3. A thirty-year-old mother of two daughters, ages twelve and nine, had died two days following being knocked out during a boxing match with another woman.

   The match was part of a "Toughman" competition staged for a TV reality show.

4. A Rhode Island mother of two was looking to "cash in" by auctioning the advertising rights to her two sons, 3 years old and 2½ months old, on eBay. Bidding was set to start at $1,500. The winning bidder would supply logo T-shirts or bibs for the

children to wear whenever they were outside their home.

5. A man who had filed a claim with the Transportation Safety Agency for the loss of his favorite belt from his luggage, had been waiting for four years for a resolution to his claim. To date, he had been unable to get a response of any kind either from the TSA or from American Airlines, despite repeated letters, faxes, and phone calls. A plea to his local Congressman resulted in an invitation for the man to become a member of the Congressman's "VIP Round Table" for a donation of $1,000.

6. The Coca-Cola Co. had admitted to rigging a marketing test for a new product, called Frozen Coke, at Burger King restaurants. The soft drink maker had made the admission after a former employee made public allegations. The former employee had since then received several death threats.

7. A girls' rugby coach had been beaten unconscious during a weekend match. Police were seeking criminal charges against several adults. "I never saw them coming," said Craig Stewart, 55, who was kicked in the head and face by parents and another coach.

8. A reporter at the *Boston Courant*, Brian Lynch, had recently uncovered widespread cheating in the Boston Public School system perpetrated not by students but by teachers and administrators. According to Lynch, teachers and principals at several schools had been changing the answers on M-CAS examinations in order to make their classes and school "pass muster" under the Kids First education reform program.

If we were to interpret these and similar news items as symptomatic of an underlying malady—as they would certainly appear to be—what might this malady be?

1. Picture if you would a washing machine on spin cycle with a load of wet towels bunched to one side.

2. Picture if you would a high-wire walker with one arm tied behind his back.

3. Picture if you would a ship on which all the cargo has shifted to port.

4. Picture if you would a teeter-totter with a 255-pound linebacker sitting on one end, and an 8-year-old girl sitting on the other.

Could it be that in America today there is a fundamental lack of balance similar to the lack of balance captured by these images, and could this lack of balance have something to do with the values we hold, and the goals we aspire to?

Let us venture a speculation.

Part 2: Half a Loaf

In his famous *Autobiography*, Ben Franklin gives us his recipe for "moral perfection:" "I included under thirteen names of virtues all that at that time occurr'd to me as 'necessary or desirable.'"

Ben's thirteen virtues for "moral perfection," mentioned previously in this volume, are as follows:

Industry	Justice
Frugality	Moderation
Order	Cleanliness
Resolution	Tranquility
Temperance	Chastity
Silence	Humility
Sincerity	

But this is a curious recipe for *"moral* perfection," is it not? In fact, wouldn't Frugality, Resolution, and Cleanliness seem to have more in common with being a "Thrifty, Brave, and Clean" Boy Scout than with being a candidate for sainthood?

Can you image the Ten Commandments including the following moral imperatives?

1. Thou shalt not be a couch potato.

2. Thou shalt not fill thy credit card unto excess.

3. Thou shalt not litter thy bedroom floor with dirty underwear.

4. Thou shalt not be lured unto procrastination.

So what kind of *"moral* perfection" is Ben advocating here anyway, with his thirteen virtues? Although Ben, the sly fox, doesn't explicitly tell us, it doesn't take us long to figure it out. Indeed, back in the 18th century, what kind of "*moral* perfection" would one need to pursue in order to ensure one's own and one's family's survival, not to mention to achieve a comfortable level of material well-being? What aspects of character would one need to develop? What kind of goals would one need to aspire to?

In fact, are not Ben's thirteen virtues—Industry, Frugality, Resolution, Order and the rest; are these not the very virtues that would all but guarantee a young man of the time—Ben's implicit audience—the proper habits of character and mind with which, firstly, to learn and excel at a trade, and, secondly, to win and keep a loyal following of patrons?

In fact, isn't Ben's recipe for "*moral* perfection" actually a recipe for *material* perfection? Interestingly, if we look closely at Ben's thirteen virtues, we notice that, in each case, the arrow of concern points inward—toward the self. Take Industry and Frugality, for example. Are we not industrious and frugal primarily, if not wholly, toward furthering our own interests (a.k.a. getting ahead)? Take Order and Resolution. Are we not orderly and resolute primarily, if not wholly, toward furthering our own interests (a.k.a. getting ahead)?

Which begs the question: Where are the natural counterparts to Ben's *inward*-directed virtues? In other words, where are the thirteen *outward*-directed virtues?

Unfortunately, Ben neglected to include these virtues in his recipe for "*moral* perfection." Had he done so, they likely would have consisted of the following or similar items:

Compassion	Forbearance
Empathy	Nurturance
Forgiveness	Fairness
Sacrifice	Loyalty
Reverence	Tolerance
Generosity	Trust
Contrition	

Every act of omission, as well as every act of commission, has consequences. What might be the consequences of Ben's having omitted the thirteen *outward*-directed virtues from his recipe for "moral perfection?" When we look at our culture today, what do we see?

Do we see "moral perfection" in the form of a balance between acquisition and contribution—between the material and the relational—between the masculine and the feminine; or do we see something more akin to a 255-pound linebacker sitting on one end of a teeter-totter, and an 8-year-old girl sitting on the other end?

Indeed, if we were to pick up a newspaper anywhere in America today, what likely would we encounter in its pages? Would we not, in fact, encounter news items very much like the ones Ben encountered in the newspaper he happened upon in the Boston Common? What about in tomorrow's edition?

The day after's edition?

Part 3: So—What Now?

Is there still time for us to right the ship—to strike a balance between the desires of self and the needs of others—between rights and responsibilities—between individualism and communitarianism—between "me" and "thee"? Or is that thumping washing machine about to fly apart; that wavering high-wire walker about to plunge into the abyss; that listing ship about to roll over and sink?

There is a refrain that runs through *Poor Richard's Lament*. It is addressed to "Good Sir" throughout, but at the very end, it is addressed to someone else: "All that might have been, all that might yet be, all is in your hands, dear reader; there is no one else."

6

Mystery Man

WE HAVE BECOME ACCUSTOMED IN OUR TIME TO A CERTAIN KIND of leader. This person actively seeks power and / or notice and is typically willing to wade deep into the conveniency of expediency (a.k.a. the swamp) in order to realize the object of his or her desire.

For example, he or she might accept large campaign donations under a tacit understanding that the donors will be rewarded in some proportionate way. Or he or she might betray a principle or a promise in order to gain an advantage judged crucial to furthering his / her ambitions. Or he or she might demonize a messenger in order to neutralize, or distract attention from, a potentially damaging truth about him or her. Or he or she might duck and weave and dissemble in the face of questioning from the media in order to avoid accountability and / or admission of malfeasance. Or he or she might spread falsehoods about current or potential rivals toward impugning their reputation and thereby diminishing their electoral prospects.

We have a special term for these leaders. We call them "politicians." Consider now, if you would, a very different kind of leader:

1. Although he was heavily involved in the founding of our nation, he never sought elected office. He was elected to various offices anyway, but on each of those occasions he was conscripted into running by people who knew what an authentic leader was and what a faux leader was not.

2. He was content to work behind the scenes and rarely took credit for his ideas or initiatives. At salons and soirées, he was mostly silent, content to listen to what other people had to say. He never allowed himself to be drawn into a public argument, and never spoke ill of anyone in public.

3. On several occasions, our mystery leader drew from his personal

fortune, or put it at risk, toward protecting or furthering the public interest. For example, in 1755, when General Edward Braddock arrived in the colonies with a large army to push the French out of the Ohio Valley, the General demanded the colonists supply him with provisions, including horses and wagons. When the colonists balked, and General Braddock threatened seizure, our mystery leader convinced the farmers of Pennsylvania to supply the General with 259 horses and 150 wagons by putting £20,000 of his personal fortune up as collateral.

When Braddock was routed by Indians allied with the French, losing to ambush after ambush two-thirds his officers and one-half his men, his own life in the bargain, our mystery leader found himself on the verge of financial ruin. Fortunately, a few months later, General Braddock's replacement, Governor Shirley of Massachusetts, covered our mystery leader's loss in full.

4. Our mystery leader refused to exploit his inventions for financial enrichment. For example, in 1741, he invented the Pennsylvania fireplace and refused to patent it. As a result, the Pennsylvania fireplace—far more efficient and effective than any heating system preceding it—proliferated throughout the land, to the comfort of many. The inventor collected not a penny.

5. Similarly, in 1749, our mystery leader invented the lightning rod and refused to patent it. As a result, the lightning rod spread to every steeple and roof top in America and Europe, saving countless people, not to mention a goodly number of farm animals, from a horrific demise. The inventor collected not a penny.

6. At the age of 42, our mystery leader retired from his printing and Almanack businesses and dedicated the rest of his life (another 42 years, it turned out) to public service. Without him in this role, the colonies would likely not have won the support of the French against the British and therefore would likely not have won the American War for Independence.

7. Our mystery leader was the very paragon of open-mindedness,
   a trait he tirelessly attempted to cultivate in others through
   his lending libraries, his Gazette, his Almanacks, his Junto, his
   College of Pennsylvania (University of Pennsylvania), his prolific
   correspondence, and his private persuasion.

One of a kind?

In truth, there are likely a thousand Benjamin Franklin's out there, right now, and as many Nelson Mandela's, and as many Martín Luther King's. The problem is that they are largely invisible, which, in most instances, is the way they want it. If we are to find them, therefore, if we are to have any chance of summoning them into public service, the way Franklin was summoned time and time again, we must seek them out.

Coffee&Dessert

1

Have You Ever Wondered...

Whether we can get fat from eating too much humble pie.

Whether we would be weightless at the center of the Earth.

Whether we're supposed to actually tell them when someone asks us "How y' doin".

Whether we can Unsubscribe to magazine inserts.

How often the average dental flosser loses track and has to start over.

Where pills go when we drop them.

Why when you get to the very end of a tube of toothpaste it takes another week to actually run out.

Why God needs to be asked to do the right thing.

Why there are about as many Democrats with hunting licenses as Republicans with PhDs.

Why the Sermon on the Mount doesn't mention anything about leaving the seat down.

Why when you look through lighted windows at night you never see anyone inside.

Why people used to disappear but now have to go to all the considerable trouble of going missing.

How many of those who talk on our cellphone in public don't have anyone on the other end.

What the proper thing to do is after sneezing into your hand.

Whether "none is" versus "none are" is a lost cause.

Whether pickup trucks ever actually pick anything up.

Why all those levers and stalks on adjustable office chairs don't seem to do anything.

Why we seem to learn more from those we disagree with than we do from those we agree with.

Why dish rags get dirty.

Whether born-agains have to be weaned all over again.

What we're agreeing to when we Accept one of those online Licensing Agreements.

What percentage of people push the coin-return button after getting their goodie from the machine.

Why God gave Adam nipples before he created Eve.

Why it takes the Jaws of Life to open a bubble-wrapped package of AAA batteries.

Why revolution is OK but evolution is not.

What the world would be like if only women could vote.

Why we don't seem to get any wiser when our wisdom teeth come in.

Whether God could create something even more powerful than he and then undo it.

Whether women have ED envy.

Why *our* prayers for a cure are answered but those of a starving mother are not.

Why global-warming deniers are so eager to advertise their ignorance.

How things might have been different had Moses delivered the "Sermon on the Mount."

Whether we would still eat cake if there were no such thing as frosting.

What will happen when whatever inflation has been inflating all these years finally gets inflated.

Which church Jesus would join.

Why it took Lincoln to free Jefferson's slaves.

What "honor thy father" means to a sexually abused daughter.

Why creatures made in the image of God are quicker to war than to forgiveness.

What would happen if a politician answered a simple yes-or-no question with a simple yes or no—and it was recorded.

If rights were sold on the open market, how much the right to be a complete and utter jerk would go for.

Why those who tell children that God punishes "bad" people by torturing them for all eternity aren't prosecuted for child abuse.

Why, if men are truly from Mars, so many of them act as if they're from Uranus.

Why, even though we all know money can't buy happiness, none of us has cancelled our order.

What the difference is between Yahweh's Great Flood and Hitler's Final Solution.

Why men wearing aprons and women wearing epaulets doesn't really solve anything.

Whether gentle giants would be gentle if they weren't giant.

Why we never sneeze when asleep or snore when awake.

How many homeless people the Pentagon would hold.

Why God chose a bunch of misogynist old geezers to spread his "Holy Word."

Why "Do the right thing" is not the first item on every agenda.

What the reward will be for the first school-bus monitor to find a child hiding under a bus.

When the last time was that a sitting U.S. President had an original idea.

Who cut down the last tree on Easter Island.

How many people have actually seen a deer with its eyes caught in headlights.

How many vegetables a vegan has to eat to be a better person.

Whether those closed weigh stations on interstates will ever open again.

Why the Second Amendment mentions militias, not schools.

Whether there is a correlation between the number of cellphone minutes spent and the amount of loneliness accumulated.

Why when we rub an ear canal with a Q-tip we can't stop.

Whether there is a parallel universe full of unmatched socks—and dropped pills.

2
What Would Happen If...

We capitalized "we" instead of "i."

Members of Congress had to wait in line.

You could sue your parents for sending you to summer camp.

If human nature was not immune to good intentions and bad legislation.

More people gave a damn than didn't.

"No Trespassing" signs had to include the phrase, "Be a good fellow."

There was an app for turning the TV off in waiting lounges.

God apologized for all those smites and smotes, not to mention all those begets and begots.

There was a Bill of Responsibilities.

Men craved chocolate more than sex.

The North seceded from the Union.

Arkie Floyd McCraw was the name of our President.

The word "politician" did not exist in any lexicon anywhere in the universe.

Jesus came out.

We had to choose between root canals and sports interviews.

Men had to sit down to pee.

Viagra was pink.

Parents could return their children for a refund.

JFK had said: "Ask not what your country can do for you, ask not what you can do for your country; ask what you can do for each other."

We defined "success" as being the best human being one could possibly be.

Narcissism was just a phase.

Men were as amenable to wearing skirts as women were to wearing pants.

The Inquisition had given out Life Achievement Awards for heroic deeds of conscience.

Eve had bargained the serpent down to a lower price.

Opera divas were anorexic; cover girls, Rubenesque.

Radical feminists tried to radical-feminize their sons.

Television had been invented by Bill Gates.

The Aztecs invaded Spain.

No one got smited or smoted or otherwise brutalized in the Old Testament.

Rip Van Winkle had slept under a Bodhi tree.

Cats barked for their food.

Picking your nose made you go blind.

Texting while driving were a capital offense.

We created our gods mostly out of the best in ourselves instead of mostly out of the worst in ourselves.

No one ran for public office in the next election.

Rachel Carson had written *Silence!*

Diamonds were a boy's best friend.

The one true God had a twin sister?

FDR had looked us all in the eye and said, "I never had sexual relations with that woman ... Eleanor Roosevelt."

Your five-year-old daughter asked you what ED meant.

Seating in both houses of Congress was by lot, not party.

There was a $5M prize for the best ethnic joke ever.

3
Oxymorons

loyal opposition	affordable housing
power sharing	holy war
high school	celebrity culture
student athlete	congressional investigation
American cuisine	moderate Republican
public servant	corporate leadership
benevolent dictatorship	Postal Service
enlightened self-interest	public trust
civil war	humble man
lifetime guarantee	safe sex
Christian Science	benign neglect
common courtesy	presidential library
angry god	customer service
semi-retired	compassionate conservative
common sense	United Nations
nonprofit	medicinal marijuana
fair share	philosopher king
smart phone	conventional wisdom
athletic scholarship	health care
government work	free love
real men	political courage
self correcting	political science
literary agent	democratic republic
short beer (male)	quick shower (female)
world leader	true story
Garden City	home work

important call

idle moment

celebratory gunfire

clean energy

political courage

government work

user friendly

private investigation

god of war

compassionate conservative

Virgin America

rush hour

religious freedom

massless particle

universal education

kingdom of God

Lady Gaga

female logic

religious education

final notice

over easy

on time

eternal bliss

urban living

satisfaction guaranteed

Facebook friend

loyal opposition

valued customer

fair tax

short break

easy setup

honest broker

American aesthetic

gun safety

Vatican bank

rock garden

self-policing

common sense

free shipping

Scientific American

world peace

male courage

amicable divorce

rock music

farm fresh

urban planning

political leaders

4

Prognostications

While communism collapsed under a mountain of red tape, capitalism will drown in an ocean of red ink.

Fundamentalism will prove to be fundamentally flawed.

Women will find the same empty pot at the end of the rainbow that men have been finding there for eons.

Designer religions will run out of Designers.

Even tech-savvy 12-year-olds will run out of the ability to keep up.

A new species of narcissus will be named after William Jefferson Clinton.

Once we finally face up to the realities of overpopulation, it will be too late.

It will be considered criminally abusive to send a child to school without a bulletproof vest on.

All the speculation at the inauguration ball of the first gay president will be about which partner leads.

Empty space will prove to be full of itself.

Airlines will start recruiting flight attendants from the World Federation of Wrestling.

Texas will be the first state since the Civil War to file for secession; there will be no objections.

Phish caught on the Internet will be sent directly to the frying pan without benefit of a herring.

Republicans will dump the elephant in order to slim down their image.

The Democrats will choose to continue to be represented by a jackass.

Nothing meaningful will be said anywhere in the world after the year 2036.

The Canada goose will be designated the official bird of the National Mall.

A clay tablet revealing the precise date of the Rapture will be discovered in the ancient ruins of Xanadu.

TV reality shows will become the only reality.

The mePhone will be the next big thing.

Women will give up on men once and for all.

Men won't notice.

5
Things Dead or Dying

humility

workmanship

self-restraint

"Made in America"

phonebooks

phys-ed

letter writing

SATs

retirement

common courtesy

just deserts

critical thinking

dead reckoning

civility

balanced budgets

solitude

wisdom

long division

newspapers

Sunday dinner

pencils

personal responsibility

cursive

personal sacrifice

decorum

quality

grammar

home cooking

pensions

yielding

simplicity

village gossip

customer always right

homework

empathy

loose change

sidewalks

"After you"

penmanship

public service

job security

liberal arts

political courage

honeybees

innocence

moderate Republicans

Catholic schools

hard news

affordable healthcare

The American Dream

unlocked churches

songbirds

leaf burning

sandlot baseball

homemade bread

hardcovers

innocence

"I do"

quiet

moral courage

nobility

air travel

conservative Democrats

common courtesy

job security

natural habitat

on time

hope

About the Author

THE AUTHOR HAS LONG FELT IN HIMSELF A SORT OF SIXTH SENSE that allows him to see things on the other side of the mountain without having to go there (see Emily Dickinson); he has long felt an inclination (drive) to share with others what he sees. At age 7, he kicked his parish priest in the shin.

An intellectual Jack-of-all-trades, Tom is a student of physics (dark matter), mathematics, law, and English composition. He has worked as a door-to-door salesman, counselor for disabled persons, corporate manager, and technical writer. During the Vietnam war era, he served as a U.S. Navy UDT/SEAL. An endorphin junkie, Tom ran the Boston Marathon three times and has swum several long-distances.

A lifelong New England resident, Tom now resides in the Pacific Northwest.

Poor Richard's Lament

SECOND EDITION
AVAILABLE IN PAPERBACK & HARDBACK

What if Ben Franklin had to come back?
What if everything depended on it?

SINCE HIS DEATH IN 1790, BENJAMIN FRANKLIN HAS BEEN CONFINED to a private apartment in the Plantation of the Unrepentant while awaiting his hearing. After repeated petitions to have his case heard, he finally is called.

Escorted to the Celestial Court of Petitions, he finds himself represented by two Intermediaries. They and Ben will plead his case, but there's a hitch. His Examiners turn out to be no other than his in-life adversaries— John Adams, Alexander Wedderburn, and Reverend William Smith.

Franklin's sins are devastatingly brought to light. For these (and there were many) Ben expects to be cast into the abyss. Surprisingly, he's granted his wish to come back to life (this time in present-day America) to witness what had become of the Founding Fathers' dream. But before that can happen, he must revisit his own past—from his birth in Boston to rabblerousing in The Colonies to his death and burial in Philadelphia.

Mystically, a secondary story moves alongside his own. Eventually, the parallel tales collide, like mammoth tectonic plates, sending out a teeth-rattling series of shocks and aftershocks. What happens next could forever upend the world.

Tom Fitzgerald's *Poor Richard's Lament* follows in the footsteps of Dickens' *A Christmas Carol*, Capra's *It's a Wonderful Life*, and Dante's *Divine Comedy*. It is an imaginative, uplifting tale of revelation and redemption, written in the legendary style of the worldy wise Benjamin Franklin, Printer.

"A grand and gorgeous book!"
MICHAEL ZUCKERMAN
University of Pennsylvania

SECOND EDITION

poor richard's lament

a most timely tale

"*A re-imagining of Benjamin Franklin you will not soon forget . . .*"

WALTER ISAACSON
author of *Benjamin Franklin: An American Life* and *Steve Jobs*

TOM FITZGERALD

acclaimed author of *Beyond Chicken Soup* and *Food 4 Thought*

the publishing CIRCLE.

Beyond 'Chicken Soup'
Toward a Life Worth All the Considerable Bother

SECOND EDITION
AVAILABLE IN PAPERBACK, HARDBACK & LARGE PRINT

Some poems are written;
others are lived.

Tom Fitzgerald's Beyond 'Chicken Soup' is for those who are unwilling to settle for shallow, easy answers of the self-help culture. This is hearty 'bread' for the mind, created for those who *want* to think in new ways, who *long* to probe beneath the surface, and who *desire* their lives that reflect a deeper wisdom.

The 'meat' of the book lies in its fifty-two sections that nourish the reader in small daily bites, allowing minds and spirits to digest little-by-little while emotionally and intellectually growing inch-by-inch.

These sections are divided into two parts: 1) an introductory reminder message concerning the nature of and/or means to "a life worth all the considerable bother;" and 2) a set of interrogatives designed to stimulate meditation, with one meditation for each day of the week. Open space follows for writing down thoughts and emotional responses that reveal where you are on the spectrum of happiness.

After all that contemplation, Fitzgerald delightfully throws in five unique and nutritious recipes for bread, all by Beth Hensperger, a James Beard Cookbook Award winner for her bestselling book, *The Bread Bible*. Bread has been a metaphor for spiritual truth for millenia. Like bread, wisdom is also taken in, chewed upon, swallowed, then digested, creating a boost of energy for spiritual growth by which we can live out our days.

Welcome to the feast!

"How did Tom Fitzgerald get inside my head
and know exactly what I needed to be told . . .
a thoughtful and thought-provoking book."
RABBI HAROLD KUSHNER
AUTHOR OF *When Bad Things Happen to Good People*

258

"How did Tom Fitzgerald get inside my head and know exactly what I needed to be told?"
RABBI HAROLD KUCHNER
author of *When Bad Things Happen to Good People*

SECOND EDITION

beyond 'chicken soup'

toward a life worth all the considerable bother

some
poems
are written;

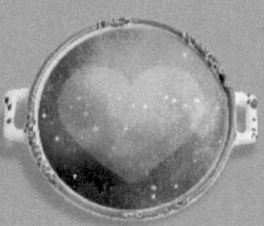

others
are lived

TOM FITZGERALD

acclaimed author of *Poor Richard's Lament*

the publishing CIRCLE.

www.ingramcontent.com/pod-product-compliance
Lightning Source LLC
Chambersburg PA
CBHW030409130626
46549CB00004B/1693

9 7 8 1 9 5 5 0 1 8 9 5 1